The *Real* Reasons Men Commit

The Real Reasons Men Commit

Why He Will—or Won't—
Love, Honor, and *Marry You*

Joel D. Block, Ph.D., and Kimberly Dawn Neumann

Avon, Massachusetts

Published by
Adams Media, an F+W Publications Company
57 Littlefield Street, Avon, MA 02322. U.S.A.
www.adamsmedia.com

ISBN 10: 1-59869-643-2
ISBN 13: 978-1-59869-643-1

Printed in the United States of America.

J I H G F E D C B A

Library of Congress Cataloging-in-Publication Data
is available from the publisher.

This publication is designed to provide accurate and authoritative information
with regard to the subject matter covered. It is sold with the understanding
that the publisher is not engaged in rendering legal, accounting, or other
professional advice. If legal advice or other expert assistance is required, the
services of a competent professional person should be sought.
    —From a *Declaration of Principles* jointly adopted by a Committee of the
American Bar Association and a Committee of Publishers and Associations

Many of the designations used by manufacturers and sellers to distinguish their
product are claimed as trademarks. Where those designations appear in this
book and Adams Media was aware of a trademark claim, the designations have
been printed with initial capital letters.

This book is available at quantity discounts for bulk purchases.
For information, please call 1-800-289-0963.

My Family and Friends: The rest is decoration.

—*Joel D. Block, Ph.D.*

For my amazing family, who taught me the
meaning of unconditional love and support.
For my friends, who feed my soul.
And, to all the women still looking for
"the one." Don't give up. . . . I haven't.

—*Kimberly Dawn Neumann*

Contents

Acknowledgments

Major thanks to Uwe Stender, our literary agent, for bringing this project to us, and for being extraordinarily responsive.

Introduction

"Beauty, will you marry me?" She answered softly, "Yes, dear Beast." As she spoke a blaze of light sprang up before the windows of the palace; fireworks crackled and guns banged, and all across the avenue of orange trees, in letters all made of fireflies, was written: Long live the prince and his bride.

—*Beauty and the Beast*

With a marriage proposal like that, it's no wonder every little girl grows up with a desire to find her own Prince Charming. But that was once upon a time. What about once upon right now? Does the modern woman need a happily-ever-after? After all, she's smart, career oriented, self-sufficient, and probably needs a man like a cricket needs an iPod. However, there's a difference between *need* and *desire*.

Finding a man to love forever is still something today's independent woman wants. Who can blame her? Love is a drug. And Mr. Right holds the promise of that profound euphoria. With him, life is full and rich and just a little bit easier to navigate. So it's a natural instinct for the single woman to be anxious to find "The One"—and get her chance at everlasting love.

Most men, however, are not in the same hurry. Even discounting female biological pressures, their timeline is quite different. For example, if a guy's already in a sexual relationship and the subject of commitment remains elusive, it's likely because he's quite content with where things stand. His girl may be great, the sex may be great, but settling down, well, that may not sound so great. As a woman, you try to rationalize this reasoning. Maybe his parents didn't read him enough fairy tales. Maybe he's a playboy at heart. Or maybe you're not "The One." In reality, he might just be happy with the way things are and figures why mess that up by promising commitment?

The truth is most single women often mistake convenient companionship and ready sex for indications that the man they're with wants a future with them. One thing women don't understand, though, is that mutual attraction doesn't always carry the same meaning for him as it does for her. To her, sex leads to love and that inevitably leads to forever (and ever). For him, sex is frequently . . . well, just sex.

Guys are not stupid. A man usually recognizes a woman won't just hop into bed with him unless he's invested in her. But men know the romantic stuff women love—flowers, candlelight dinners, heartfelt e-mail exchanges—and use it as foreplay. So, he may appear invested, or even be invested to an extent—but it doesn't mean he's committed.

So how do you know if you're on the road to forever when it's clearly a slippery slope between convenience and commitment? Of course you're going to want to believe in the fairy-tale ending if you're with a man who seems to be sending all the right signals. And there is nothing wrong with that. But, wouldn't it be nice to be able to discern between a real Mr. Right and the frequently encountered Mr. Not-Right-Now?

Introduction

The Real Reasons Men Commit is an honest look at what's happening in the minds of men when facing the subject of "future." It's a detailed guide to separating the real thing from the dead-end relationships that steal your time, sap your energy, and leave you single and (*ugh*) still searching.

Your guides for facing your future are a male and female team. Joel D. Block, Ph.D., is an award-winning psychologist and author of nearly twenty books on love and sex. He knows the male psyche. Even more important, he specializes in dealing with sexuality and relationships in his very active practice and answers dozens of e-mails around the issue of commitment nearly every week.

Kimberly Dawn Neumann is a popular New York City-based dating/sex/relationship writer who has also worked extensively on Broadway (making her privy to more than a little relationship drama). She and her friends have been in the trenches. Some have found true love; others are still looking. But all of them agree that when it comes to commitment, there is a difference between the men who will speak of future and mean it, and the boys who are still messing around. In writing this book, she hopes to elucidate how to spot a keeper.

Between them, Joel and Kimberly bring two important perspectives—the man who's an expert on men and relationships, and the woman who's been in your shoes (and nearly worn them out). Together they've fleshed out what will lead a man to commit, and view it as a positive step in his life rather than the acquisition of a ball-and-chain.

The truth is that sometimes men are actually confused about the realities of commitment. They may be commit-prone, but simply need some coaching to fortify their courage. Once you learn to spot the signs, you'll be better able to determine if you should stay with a relationship and view his ambivalence as a passing phase, or recognize that it's time to move on.

The Real Reasons Men Commit was designed to address the questions you keep asking yourself: *Can he commit to me? Is this just sex, a bookmark in his life, or the real thing that just needs a little encouragement? What is the best approach to cultivate a commitment-oriented mindset?* The good news is that there are definitive answers and soon you'll be better able to tell the difference between a guy with cold feet and one stuck in an intractable single-forever stance.

1

COMMITMENT
and the Common Man

*H*itting it off with a new man is thrilling—especially if he's handsome, funny, and not a distant relative of Ted Bundy. When the initial attraction resonates deeper and you find that you actually *like* the guy, even better! You come to spend more and more time with each other. You start dating. And after awhile, you begin entertaining the idea that this relationship might actually be going somewhere. But where exactly, and when?

You don't want to be single forever; dating loses its appeal. You want something permanent. You want to be "in it" with a partner. Bottom line: You want a commitment.

Commitment is not a fleeting, lust-driven state. In fact, it's just the opposite. More obvious during hard times than in the rush of passion, commitment isn't really tested until infatuation wears off. You're seeking more than that special somebody; you want that special somebody who's in it for the long haul—even after the sizzle fizzles and the companionship is more comfortable than energized.

Truth be told, we've put a lot of thought into what fuels commitment issues. Our conclusion? Fear is merely the surface manifestation of much deeper emotions that hinder

1

long-term relationships. When the guy you are interested in is unable to entertain the idea of "commitment," it's probably not just about you, the timing, or whatever other excuse he may have given you. The more likely culprits? Vulnerability and his abject distaste for emotional instability.

....

The Panic Sprint

Consider Peter, a man in his mid-thirties who broke an engagement three years ago. Now, engaged once again, he's feeling the urge to run a second time.

I don't know how to explain it, but I just can't get as relaxed with Michelle as I did at the beginning of our relationship. Now it goes something like this: Michelle comes over and I am sitting there watching some stupid program on TV. I'm not really even watching; I'm just staring at the TV. This is my way of avoiding my feelings when I'm not in a good place emotionally. She looks at me and asks what's wrong. Interesting, she can read me without me saying a word.

My fiancé is asking me what is going on, she cares. The sensible thing would be to tell her that I'm feeling lousy, that my knee hurts, and that I'm worried about how things are going at work. But I don't react sensibly. I say, "Nothing, I'm fine." She gives it another try. "You sure, what's up?" Once again, I give her the nonresponse, response. This time it's a mumble, "Nothing. Nothing's up. I'm just watching a program." Then she goes for broke. "It doesn't sound like nothing's up and everything's fine. You seem upset about something. Talk to me!"

You would think I would let it out, but I don't give an inch. Something holds me back and I don't even know what it is. There's just something that I can't get past. And as if that isn't bad enough, she wants to be closer to me and I'm thinking how much of a shit I'm gonna be if I break this engagement.

What Peter doesn't realize is that his behavior is not atypical. He's blaming himself for not communicating. He can feel himself closing off. He clearly cares for his fiancé but he can't figure out what's going on in his head. But instead of dealing with it, he starts to panic and considers fleeing rather than facing whatever is causing his unease. Some people would see this as a classic case of *commitment-phobia.*

....

It's actually *vulnera-phobia*—the fear of vulnerability—which strikes directly at the heart of the commitment issue. Vulnerable literally means "able to be wounded." In common usage we refer to being vulnerable when we're feeling fragile and emotionally penetrable. In medical parlance the word is often used when a patient's immune system is compromised and he or she is particularly susceptible to illness. In "male speak" vulnerability is defined as weakness and that is certainly not something with which they wish to be associated.

In fact, most males regard feeling vulnerable as the kiss of death. If you asked any man, regardless of occupation, if he would volunteer to feel and appear vulnerable, he is likely to opt for a root canal instead. Women, on the other hand, are socialized to more readily accept vulnerability. Case in point, women are allowed to get emotional during "chick flicks," while many men would probably deny they'd ever related to one, let alone even seen one (unless they were dragged there by a woman). Therefore, the idea that a man might not want to commit for fear of showing fallibility probably wouldn't immediately cross a woman's mind. But it should. The very answer to encouraging commitment may lie in the recognition of this trait.

Be a Man!

Despite their macho brawn, men are definitely the weaker sex. They may talk louder and act tougher, but most of them are scared little boys. They're much more lost than women when it comes to knowing who they are and what they feel. That's because they've been taught not to think about or discuss these things. And in a love affair, they're at a *real* disadvantage. When they're in love, they get totally confused, caught in the classic approach/avoidance conflict. *I love being with her, but . . .* This is why they often withdraw and run away when relationships are taken to the next level.

....

The Female Endurance Event

Here is what Michelle, Peter's fiancé, had to say:

Peter is just so frustrating to me. I don't need to know every detail of his life. I don't have time for every detail. And I don't bore him with the minutiae of my own life. But it is the real stuff that goes on with him that I want to know about. I want him to be able to tell me when something is not right, when he's worried about something, when something is bothering him—like committed couples are supposed to do. I want the kind of openness that we had when we first got involved. Instead, as the relationship has progressed, he's become more guarded. I feel like we're less connected now that we're engaged. I thought we had a future, but now I'm not so sure.

Why does Peter's vulnerability index rise in relation to Michelle becoming more central to his life? The operative word is *central*. Michelle's life is beginning to revolve around Peter. He has become her constant, the part of her life that is familiar. The irony is that as Peter becomes more important to Michelle's life, the stakes get higher and the fear of losing Peter's validation weighs greater.

. . . .

This is where men begin to have second thoughts—they sense dependence setting in, and along with that, the dreaded feeling of vulnerability creeps up, big-time. And then, thoughts of bailing enter. *But women experience dependence and vulnerability too and we don't bail as readily,* you argue. Fair point. Lots of women know what it means to feel vulnerable. But keep in mind most men have been socialized differently.

Consider the media by which men have been conditioned—from Hercules to James Bond, the heroic man is presented as impenetrable. You can witness this in everyday life with the different reactions to male and female children in the same situations. A shy little girl is considered cute; a shy boy is thought of as a sissy. A frightened girl is comforted; a frightened boy is told to act like a man. Girls are allowed to cry openly without shame; boys who even shed a tear are open to ridicule. This suggests that this stoic, Clint Eastwood-esque male composure may be a defense against feeling emotionally vulnerable.

Men are drawn to heroes like Hercules, James Bond, and Eastwood's various roles because unconsciously they represent a fantasy that is compelling. It's the wish to avoid feeling out of control, to avoid that anxious, shaky experience—the kind of experience that many people feel speaking in front of a group for the first time. As one man aptly put it, "Feeling dependent on someone reminds me of having to give a speech in my English class. As I was walking to the front of my class I felt defenseless, like a lamb led to slaughter."

So, if men have been programmed not to open up, what are you supposed to do?

Don't Make Excuses for Him

If getting him to commit is your goal, the first thing you'll need to do is stop giving him a "free pass." In other words, quit allowing him to make excuses for his poor behavior, or coming up with your own excuses for it.

This may be hard if you're a woman prone to pathological empathy, which means you take "poor baby, he needs understanding" over the top. If you catch yourself saying, "He'll come around, he's just shy," "He wants to commit, he just needs time," or "He doesn't call because he's on the phone for work all day," you may be enabling his avoidance tendencies.

In its more severe form, a guy doesn't even have to offer an excuse or explanation for being inconsiderate; his girlfriend will come up with explanations that he never even considered. Pathological empathy is about being *too* understanding to the point where it can be ridiculous. "He forgot my birthday because he's been busy painting his apartment." Sounds absurd, but if you let yourself be blinded by your desire for a committed relationship, you might just catch such irrational excuses unexpectedly popping out of your mouth. Before it gets that far, take stock of your own empathic tendencies by asking yourself the following questions:

1. Am I constantly trying to explain my boyfriend's actions (or lack of action) to my friends?
2. Do I look for qualities in my boyfriend that I can later pin his mannerisms on (i.e., "He wasn't close to his father growing up so he has trouble expressing his feelings now")?
3. Do I frequently catch myself feeling sorry for my boyfriend because I know how hard it is for him to be open with me?
4. Am I allowing him to forget important dates or things we have planned together by blaming his forgetfulness on the other pressures in his life?
5. Do I frequently hear myself saying to him "It's okay, I understand" about everything?

If you answer "yes" to three or more of the previous questions, you may be hindering your own chances at a happy ending by not making your man take responsibility for his own actions. And yes, that is a problem. If there is one thing all single women need to understand, it's this: It's not about what he says; it's about what he *does*. As the saying goes, *actions speak louder than words*.

To elucidate this point, consider the case of Jennifer, a thirty-something woman who called her boyfriend to tell him that her apartment had been broken into. He responded by saying how sorry he was. His tone was remorseful. He was sincerely interested in the details of what had transpired, asking a bevy of questions like: *Are you okay? Did you call the police? How did they get in? What did they steal?* But even though he lived just a half-hour away, he didn't jump in his car and come over to comfort her. Instead, he ended the conversation first because he had to get going. . . . He was late meeting his former college friend at a nearby bar. In this case, his actions clearly trumped his words.

Yet Jennifer remembers making excuses for him. It was one of his closest friends, after all, and they hadn't seen each other in a while. And well, she was okay—it was not like she was left bound and gagged. And besides, the robber only took her crappy DVD player. Her attempt at exempting her boyfriend's behavior didn't take away the feelings that she had inside, though. She was angry, sad, and disappointed that her boyfriend didn't come through for her. She had been *robbed*. It's not like there was a bug in her kitchen that she'd called him to come over and kill. This was serious! She needed him. And, his actions let her down. But she allowed him to get away with it by behaving like a pathological empathic.

Lesson learned? From now on, no matter what you do, always consider commitment an action rather than an idea. Look at what he does—don't just listen to his words. Effective actions demonstrate commitment; words are just words. If he's truly committed, he doesn't need to talk about it; he shows it. When a man is ready to commit, you'll know because he will start *behaving* in a fashion consistent to that role of boyfriend/fiancé/partner. And you'll notice that you've stopped having excuse-making conversations with yourself—there'll be no reason.

Will He or Won't He?

A lot of times when you're in the thick of a relationship, it's difficult to see things clearly or as they truly are—especially if you're hoping that this guy is truly *it*. He might be or he might not be. So you want to be sure he is before you waste any more time and energy.

Bear in mind, getting close to another person is a scary and time-consuming thing. You have to open yourself up and make yourself vulnerable. You must make the space for the other person to open up to you and make an effort to understand him. It's not supposed to be comfortable. It's supposed to be significant, meaningful, and a process.

Truthfully, there is no guarantee. Success in dating and marriage, as with most things in our world, is subject to probability—there are no "sure things". But if commitment is your goal, you want the probabilities stacked in favor of marriage. Short of a crystal ball, it's the best way to guarantee your relationship will last through time. So where should you start? Well, from the get-go you need to learn to pay attention to the red flags that suggest your potential forever man may be a poor choice for the future. Some men are just not ready, and some will never be—even if they get married, they will not commit their heart.

The First Date: Spotting the Top Ten Red Flags

You should start being alert on the first date. Why? Because you don't want to get involved with someone who immediately has you making excuses for him, or someone with whom a relationship is likely to go nowhere. If you're looking to avoid these situations, there are definite red flags that you should keep an eye out for—and if you see them waving on a first or second date, know it's time to bolt for the exit!

So what are these flags? They're signs that he's not willing or able to have a committed relationship. Be very aware if your new potential partner says or implies any of the following ten things in your early dates:

1. "I've had a bad marriage and a crazy divorce, and don't ever want to be hurt again."
2. "I've had so many bad relationships and been rejected so many times in the past that I feel hesitant to take that chance again."
3. "Did you know that 50 percent of all marriages end in divorce? Makes you never want to take the plunge, right?"
4. "In almost every relationship I've been in, sooner or later the woman became too demanding of me and my time."
5. "I don't let other people have power over my happiness or control me. I don't like being told what I have to do."
6. "Being in love makes you act like a fool and not in a good lovesick way but more of an 'I'm totally out of control' way."
7. "Love equals marriage plus bills plus responsibility—and that's so limiting!"
8. "Being in love makes a person so dependent and needy. Seriously, who wants to be joined at the hip?"
9. "Aren't all relationships really just for sex? Why complicate things with emotional attachment?"
10. "I think when you get in a serious relationship you lose your independence and sense of self."

When you consider what's behind these statements—fear of being hurt, fear of losing control, fear of responsibility—it's hard to avoid coming to an obvious conclusion. For the most part, these are guys who would rather be shot in the face than have to wrestle with their fear of feeling or even appearing vulnerable. They are not emotionally available and, consequently, are a big gamble when it comes to commitment.

Of course, it's ultimately your choice to get involved with a man who throws up such flags. You are doing so at your own risk. Let's say you recognize only one flag on your first date and, after being brutally honest with yourself, you still see this guy as a possibility. Then you might choose to go on a second date or even a third. Your gut instinct is important, but since you've noticed one of these flags on an early date, you absolutely must keep on the lookout for additional signs. In other words, don't decide that he's passed and then continue on blindly. Always keep your eyes wide open.

Moving Forward:
Tough Questions to Ask Yourself

So you've made it past the initial phase and red flags are not flapping in the wind. Does that mean you're home free? *No way!* Again, focusing on commitment as the goal, it's now time to ask yourself some important questions about how this guy stacks up. Keep in mind that in order to answer thoughtfully, there will have to be some time and energy invested into this relationship. When you are ready, your responses to the following will give you important insight into where things are heading.

Is he MIA when you need him—not just in words, but in actions as well? If you are the one always doing things for him and jumping through hoops to win his love, this is not a commitment-worthy relationship. This guy is likely protecting himself from experiencing vulnerability. Men who fear feeling or appearing vulnerable are quite typically takers, not givers. If he doesn't have a desire to please you, it's more likely about convenient sex, not commitment. Furthermore, if it does result in marriage, it will only get worse.

Does he usually blame others for his problems and see himself as the victim? If he chronically points the finger at everyone else, he's got a major maturity issue and that usually makes him a relationship risk. Immature men don't have the inner strength needed to deal with feeling vulnerable and when the going gets tough, they bail. These men don't have a firm sense of who they are and consequently fear they will lose themselves if they merge into a partnership (which is what the word *commitment* implies to them). This may seem incredibly infantile and even insulting to women. But men who have not clearly defined themselves worry that if they fall in love and stay with one woman, they will somehow lose their manhood.

Is he very critical of you? If you feel inadequate around him or are afraid his love for you is based on your looks (for example, he pays too much attention to what you eat, fearing you'll gain weight), then this is a man who is not ready for a real-life relationship. He's looking for a fantasy. Since men have so much trouble talking about their feelings, the commitment-phobic types are frequently caught up in the search for the "perfect" woman. This way they can avoid getting too close in any relationship (thus making themselves vulnerable) by deciding that things aren't right and that she's not "perfect." Instead of facing their own issues, these men find it easier to blame you, leave, and start over with someone new.

Does his lack of the "disclosure gene" have him internalizing everything? Men spend their whole lives showing that they're strong, ignoring the want to disclose personal feelings. They fight for independence the way women struggle to connect. This need to appear unflappable, however, can make them hesitant to show their true feelings. Though you don't need an *"Oprah* moment" every day of your relationship, you do need a man who is willing to be there for you and be honest about his emotions. Therefore, when looking at a long-term prospect, it is important to discern if he is reasonably generous and truthful with his feelings. Men who are unwilling to express their inner-selves allow issues to compound until they seem insurmountable. And as soon as these relationship issues become overwhelming, this type of man will typically take flight.

Is his own pleasure the most motivating factor in his life? If a man is unbending and working from the mindset that his being happy and satisfied is the most important part of the relationship, he is not only going to be unable to commit, he's also not going to satisfy you. It's one thing to look out for your best interest—that's healthy—but it's another thing to be plain selfish. When you look out for your best interest, you still take other's needs into consideration. Selfishness ignores the other person, and it is sure to create an overflowing reservoir of anger. Remember, you're looking for a partnership, and that implies someone has your pleasure in mind as well

Is he an immature boy pretending to be a man? A man overly concerned about image is likely to have the anti-commitment belief: "I can do whatever I want without reporting to anybody." Of course, men know they'll have to make concessions in a relationship. But men who lack a grown-up attitude become a bit panicked. They worry that a relationship means they'll have to account to their women all the time and be locked in by promises and agendas. They also fear looking like they're "whipped," or at their girlfriend's beck and call, to their buddies (with whom they assume they won't get to hang out anymore). This negative view of what a relationship means prevents this type of guy from even considering a real future with a woman.

Does he not have a strong set of standards or beliefs to live by? A committed man should keep his word and play it straight. If his character is questionable, eventually he will betray you. Infidelity is simply too easy for a man who is prone to shortcuts and lacks integrity. Also, being unfaithful is one of the main ploys used by vulnera-phobic men. By weakening their commitment through cheating they limit feeling vulnerable in their primary relationship.

Does he bad-mouth the concept of marriage? If a man takes other people's marriages lightly, or is cynical about people getting divorced or his friends cheating on their wives, it's less likely he's going to commit to a long-term relationship of his own. While he may pretend to act jaded about it or knock the institution, in actuality it could be a cover for the fact that he's scared to let himself be that susceptible to being hurt.

If you answer "yes" to any or all of the above, you may be dealing with a truly self-serving and inconsiderate man. Unfortunately what typically happens in this type of situation is that the woman falsely believes she will be the one to change him. So, she does all she can to meet her man's needs in an effort to keep the relationship moving forward. And this usually works for a while because he's happy. But he'll also become accustomed to things going his way. And the minute she asks for more of a commitment, he'll take off in search of that imaginary woman who will nurture his needs without expecting anything in return.

How Not to Scare Him Off

Are you beginning to think that you'll never find a good man? Don't. That's not the case at all. You will, but you need to understand how men perceive their vulnerability and what you can do to diffuse that scary impulse for them. The first thing to comprehend is that men are constantly on the lookout for signs that trigger their I'm-going-to-feel-exposed reaction. On the flip side, they are so busy trying to protect themselves they probably won't notice when you float subtle signals that allow them to relax in your presence.

A woman who understands this can make gestures—many of them symbolic, like nodding to show understanding and validating rather than debating his emotional disclosures—that cost nothing and will make her man feel safe and secure, but also strong. In other words, pay attention to what's bubbling below the surface of your guy's commitment issues and you'll be at a major advantage. Here are some tips for moving a man away from commitment-phobia.

1. When you first meet, don't ask him a bunch of resume questions. Do you really need to know how long he's been at his job, or if he owns or rents before you decide if you like him on a personal level? Also, don't grill him about his future prospects. In general, praise him for what he is—not what he's achieved or plans on achieving.

2. Do not come off as desperate. Nothing will send a man running like the feeling that he's there because of a woman's biological clock or because he's filling a job opening for your husband.

3. When he mentions that he wants to go out with the guys, don't make a face. Simply tell him to have a good time. Same thing goes for not scaring him with too many group events he *must* attend too quickly (i.e. weddings, friend's birthday parties, etc.). The idea is to let him get used to you being in his life without a fear of you taking it over.

4. Guys treasure their own freedom, but they expect you to be totally loyal from almost the first minute you meet. In fact, men can grow secretly jealous of your former lovers, guys at your office, or basically any man in your life. Diffuse this vulnerability by speaking well of him in public, or making sure you don't accidentally undercut his masculinity by pointing out his faults (which will weaken his commitment).

note: Be aware that some women go too far, offering too much loyalty too fast and then becoming angry at themselves or at their man. You have the right to have lunch with a male coworker or stay friends with an ex. You don't have to undermine your own relationships in order to affect his loyalty. Just make sure you're honest about your plans, and build up your current beau simultaneously.

5. Guys are heavily invested in appearing strong—the diametric opposite of vulnerable. The big secret here

is that he also wants you to love him as a sensitive, fragile soul. If you recognize this fact, you can let him act big and strong in public, but feel free to nurture him a little bit behind closed doors for example, stroke his hair or skin gently while you talk to him. He'll subconsciously start to sense you get him and won't know why.

6. Despite the popular books suggesting that you play hard to get, we feel that is precisely the wrong thing to do. Yes, you'll draw his interest for a while. But even as he pursues you, there is a part of him that resents it—you are making him feel vulnerable. Playing by these types of tricky rules and gaming him, making him jealous, will only push him further from commitment.

By now you should be starting to see the problem. Men don't like to feel vulnerable, but women can inadvertently make them feel that way. When that happens there is a disconnect, which is unfortunate since both men and women really do want the same thing (read: *love*). In Chapter 2 we'll explore why many people today find themselves in a commitment quandary, and how both sexes see the future—not on Mars or Venus, but right here on planet Earth.

THE COMMITMENT-READY MAN . . . Is okay with the fact that giving his heart to a woman might make him feel vulnerable. Once he accepts that vulnerability is part of an intimate relationship, he'll be more willing to risk inviting you into his life for the long term.

The
COMMITMENT
Conundrum

Times have changed. Dates are easily and readily found online. Foreplay includes text messaging. Waiting for marriage before having sex has all but gone the way of the typewriter. Living together before marriage is commonplace. The average age women are marrying is climbing. And commitment is somehow supposed to fall somewhere between the first date and the reading of the vows.

You want a commitment, but do you know what that means for you in today's dating culture? And what his version of commitment entails? Are you ready to find out?

Once upon a time, or even recently in the premarital land of your parents, commitment meant one thing—a ring on the left hand. And for many people, that's still the real deal. But there are also a million shades of gray between living single and being married. Some people manage to stay happily together their entire lives without ever walking down the aisle. Other couples take the marital plunge only to be desperately seeking an annulment almost as soon as the honeymoon is over. So, what's the status of the pledge today?

The answer to that question is up to you. The more important question to ask yourself is: *Do I need the security that comes from being in a committed relationship? And what constitutes commitment for me?* And, unfortunately, we can't answer that for you—nor can your mom, best friend, brother, sister, coworker, or whomever. You are the only person who can decide what will make you happy. So before you go projecting commitment ideas upon a potential mate, make sure you've really devoted some thought to your commitment vision.

That said, there are societal pressures and norms that you have to deal with concerning the subject. As does he! Don't forget, it takes two to dance the commitment tango. In order to better understand how the both of you will face commitment issues in this day and age, we've done some trend-spotting to see what people think.

Women and Commitment

Consider the idea of living your life alone. Would it be *that* bad? You could fill your days with your career, hobbies, travel, friends, and family. And knowing the average woman, it would be a very full and interesting life. Just look at the crew from *Sex and the City*. Carrie Bradshaw and gang certainly made the most of their single status while they had it. Shoes, clothes, cocktails, parties, brunches, art showings—they had a plethora of things to keep them busy and happy.

Yet, like the *SATC* ladies (especially Charlotte), the average woman, probably still thinks something is missing if she's not yet found "The One." That's because as a female, you're probably anything but vulnera-phobic. Women are more accepting of the fact that they may feel vulnerable in their lives. And so they learn to deal with that emotion. On the flip side, however, the thing that worries them is a lack of security. And an obvious way to find that comforting feeling? Hand in hand with a man, of course.

Think about it. Women today are strong, smart, and independent. They can take care of themselves. But even the most powerful women don't like to feel as if they're flying completely solo. A woman wants someone to hug her. A man who will put his arms around her and make her feel safe and protected. It's not about giving up control; it's about feeling supported. Why else would today's power women still be looking for a partner if not for the companionship, the support, and the love? To women, being in a committed relationship is not the end of their freedom; it is the definition of it.

Once a woman has a significant other, she can relax. It's one less pressure in her life, one area where she no longer has to try and prove herself. By societal standards, women today are supposed to have it all. Yet, there is still an insecurity and fear that they're somehow missing out if they don't have someone to come home to. People begin to wonder, "Why hasn't she found someone?" And soon she starts to wonder the same thing. Never mind that she is carrying the workload of a man, paying her own rent, striving to stay in great shape, and trying to maintain close relationships with friends and family. Society expects her to find someone and somehow views it as sad if she doesn't have a man in her life.

But societal pressures are usually not the real reason a woman wants to find a mate. It's not so much to fit in or to keep up appearances as it may be (though some women admittedly do get caught up in the quest for the "rock"). Typically, it's more about a yearning for a partner, someone to help share the load. And the prospect of having children aside, it's about finding security.

Additionally, even in the modern world, women are still looking for a bit of the fairy tale. And it's okay, you can admit it. We think you should! There is nothing wrong with being a romantic at heart. Every day, people get to experience the giddiness of love and a supportive, amazing relationship. So, why can't you? And we agree—you should. But the point here is more than that—we want to know what women think of commitment.

The answer? By and large, the large number of women we spoke with think it is a wonderful thing. And though personal interpretations may vary, most women are looking for something long term. Sure, you can be in a committed short-term relationship, which might be quite lovely, but it has an expiration date. When speaking of commitment, the majority of women equate that with long lasting (i.e., marriage). Otherwise, you're still "dating," "on the market," or worse yet, "taken but technically single."

Commitment also implies exclusivity. Most women don't like to share. They want a man who is theirs and theirs alone. It's once again about security. Women don't want to have to fight for male attention all their lives. And if they want children, they want a man who will be exclusively theirs throughout the entire process (not just to sew the seed, so to speak).

Bottom line: A commitment says, "I love you, and it is you and me together forever"—and whether men like it or not, that promise is what most women want.

Men and the C Word

Yes, the C word. It says it all. While women can use the word "commitment" with a smile on their face, for many men, forming those three syllables into something coherent can be a major challenge. That's not to say all men dread the

C word, but it does invoke a positively visceral reaction for many—especially the vulnera-phobic.

But why is that? There are certainly many happily married men in today's society. Plenty of men cherish their wives, love their families, and had no problem getting to "I do." What is it that makes some men eager to couple and makes others balk at the idea?

One answer lies in the perceived definition of commitment. While commitment-ready men and women can readily identify the benefits of having a committed partner, the I-just-can't-say-it male is stuck on the idea that a permanent coupling means the end of life as he knows it. Instead of looking at the positives, the vulnera-phobic male sees the word *commitment* as holding nothing but negative connotations.

And there has definitely been societal perpetuation of this stereotype. Just look at all the sitcoms on TV that are built around wives nagging their husbands, and these men lamenting the "good ol' days" when they were bachelors. While that kind of storyline might make for funny programming, in our heavily media-influenced society, it delivers the wrong message about relationships to men. The guys in these shows look weak to the commitment-phobic male. They have a woman running their lives and making all their decisions and it's not surprising that a single man might find himself thinking, *No way in hell do I want a relationship like that!*

Consequently, he shies away from a serious relationship, or he seeks his own definition of "commitment." This is where things get murky. In an effort to protect themselves and shield their vulnerability, many men find alternate ways to cope with the word. His watered-down version of commitment probably doesn't involve him saying "I do." Instead he might say, "Here is a set of my keys," which the commitment-hopeful woman will take as a sign that they're in it for the long haul. But it might just be his way of pseudo-committing—committing to not wanting to lose her, but not technically committing *to* her. Keep in mind, locks can always be changed.

COMMITMENT INACTION

Let's say you meet a single, straight, and interested guy named Bennett, who his friends call Benny. He invites you to call him Benny within minutes of meeting. He makes you laugh, and listens to what you have to say. You agree to meet up some more, and learn he's stressed about the ad campaign he's working on, but he still makes time for you. No more lonely nights, right?

Fast-forward a few months. Now things are changing. He seems too tired to get together as often, so you ask, "Benny, where is this relationship going?" You ignore the warning of his wince, and try not to notice that he appears weak-kneed as he stammers a reply, "I don't want to lose you."

"Are we *it* forever?" you ask.

"We're *it*, forever," he says. His words soothe your soul.

Another few months go by. Secretly you are beginning to doubt that you and Benny are really *it* forever. *It* seems to be only when it's convenient for him—and nowadays it appears he's losing interest in *it*. He doesn't call when he knows you want him to, and he avoids making plans more than three or four days in advance. But the good times are great, you reason—though you're not having them so often anymore.

You ask your girlfriend, Ginny, "Is he committed, or just using me for convenient sex and company when he has nothing better to do?" She says, "I've been trying to answer that question in my own life for some time now, and it's difficult. Who knows? Maybe he just has trouble settling down."

"But I want something to happen *soon*," you stress. "I know guys have a hard time climbing the commitment ladder. Each step is an ordeal. But still . . ."

"Why not just ask him again," Ginny offers optimistically. "Maybe he'll tell you he's had his concerns and he's past that. You'll feel greatly relieved."

You pause. You want to believe her. "Okay, yeah, I'm gonna."

A week passes, and then two more. Ginny asks if you have asked again. You haven't. "Go ahead," she prompts. "Do it."

"But I can't let him know my doubt!" you fire back. "Besides, what if he says he really likes the idea of having a pillow pal, and nothing more? Maybe I'll find out that he doesn't really want to be married, but can't bring himself to tell me. The thought of starting over makes me want to vomit!"

"But if you don't ask," Ginny insists, "you'll waste your time with him. I know, I've done it more than once, and then when I face another birthday alone, I beat myself up."

Ginny calls back a few minutes later with a confession. Despite her advice, in contrast to everything she's said, she is just as confused when it comes to the commitment thing as ever.

The disconnect here happens because women tend to view commitment as permanence. But commitment-shy men can't handle that concept. The idea of giving up their independence is unequivocally viewed as a loss without consideration of the fact that a loving relationship might more than compensate for any concessions made in that department.

Men are also at an advantage when it comes to getting away with this behavior: our culture supports it! Whereas a single woman might be judged with a comment like "Oh, she must be so lonely" if she's not with someone, a man can be exonerated with a simple "Well, he's capitalizing on his virile years isn't he?" And that statement might even be followed by a knowing chuckle. The "player" is often esteemed by other men and excused by women. The truth? He's being enabled. He has no need to commit because society views his status as acceptable—if not preferable.

That said, not every man is a rascal that refuses to commit. So, what are the characteristics of the man who drags his heels? That is a very good question and, fortunately, we managed to dig up some answers.

How Do *You* Define Commitment?

Know what you're looking for before you impress your ideals of commitment upon a potential mate. Use these questions to determine your definition of commitment.

1. When you say you want a commitment, are you satisfied with a domestic partner agreement? Or do you want the ring, the wedding, the whole shebang?
2. What do you consider acceptable as far as sex in your relationship? Are you okay with an "open" marriage? Or do you expect absolute fidelity? Something in between?
3. Are you okay with waiting for your partner to feel financially secure before he proposes, or do you need someone who is ready to talk future with you right now?
4. Are you ready to be with just one man for the rest of your life, or do you still have some oats left to sow (be honest with yourself)?
5. What are your reasons for wanting a man to commit? Is it just to keep up with your friends (You don't want to be the last one left unmarried)? Are you desperate for a child? Or are you looking for a partner with whom to grow old and enjoy life?

What Makes a Man Skittish

It took a while for it to happen, but as divorce rates continued to climb and the sociological idea of "relationship" shifted, the academic set finally got interested in studying commitment. Now, thanks to several studies from the National Marriage Project at Rutgers University, there are stats to back up what women have always surmised—if a man avoids commitment conversations there are definite reasons. And not surprisingly, we were able to link a touch of vulnera-phobia to all of them.

The first study from the National Marriage Project managed to identify ten key traits that could be associated with the man who was not prepared to walk down the aisle. To help you understand the mind of the I'm-not-ready man, we figured we should take a closer look. Here are the top ten reasons cited for a man who won't marry (and how vulnera-phobia manifests in each):

He can get sex without marriage more easily than in the past. Once upon a time, the only way to get a woman into bed was by putting a ring on her finger. *Oh how times have changed.* Women have discovered their sexual selves, but at the same time this liberation may have also inadvertently undermined their commitment wishes. The good news? They have more interesting sex lives. The bad news? They may have a harder time getting what they want *out* of bed. This also gives the vulnera-phobic man a perfect out because as soon as he feels himself getting too close to a woman, he can split and satisfy his sexual needs elsewhere.

He can enjoy the benefits of having a wife by cohabitating rather than marrying. Why buy the milk when you already have the cow, or something like that . . . ? Living together prior to marriage has become more and more accepted over the years. In fact, according to U.S. Bureau of the Census data, there are more than 5 million unmarried couples currently shacking up in the United States alone. Problem is, while women think this may be a step toward marriage, the studies don't support that hope. In fact, research done by Scott Stanley, co-director of the Center for Marital and Family Studies at the University of Denver, indicates that men who live with their girlfriends and then marry them tend not to be as faithful to the union. For vulnera-phobic men, the cohabitation option is ideal because they get most of the benefits but still feel like they have their freedom too. Why on earth would they want to get married when they've already got what they want?

He wants to avoid divorce and its financial risks. Single men are worried about their money disappearing as soon as they get in a serious relationship, which is odd when you consider that most women today are perfectly capable of pulling down a solid income themselves. Still, men worry that if they commit, their funds will disappear. And worse yet, if things go kaput, they don't want to lose their hard-earned income to divorce settlements and alimony payments. So rather than risk their wage, they figure it's easier not to commit at all. The ironic thing, however, is that married couples tend to actually make *more* money as a duo. But, for the commitment-phobic man, the lack of guarantee is enough to convince him not to take the risk.

He wants to wait until he's older to have children. A woman's biological clock is set much earlier than that of a man. This makes it much easier for men to play the "not ready for kids" card. Why? A man over forty can snag a woman of childbearing age and still have children. The reverse? Not so easy. So, a vulnera-phobic male can get out of a committed situation by saying, "Well, she wanted kids right now and I wasn't ready." How long can he use that excuse? Unfortunately for the female gender, until he starts shooting blanks, which could be a very long time.

He fears that marriage will require too many changes and compromises. No more PlayStation at 2 A.M.? No more bar-hopping with the boys? No more sleeping in on the weekends? No way! Single men who are shying away from relationships are likely to focus on all the things they'll have to give up if they commit. For the vulnera-phobic male, just the thought of having to alter his life freaks him out. Seriously, what makes a person more vulnerable than change? Marriage requires that he be a man. And the idea of having to be responsible may actually be more than many of the commitment-shy boys out there can handle.

He is waiting for the perfect match and she hasn't yet appeared. And you thought you were the only one waiting for your ideal match. Guess again. Men are actually hoping to find someone to complete them as well (as sappy as that sounds). The difference with the vulnera-phobic man, however, is that he can always pick fault with anyone he's dating if he gets too close for comfort and simply say, "Well, you aren't my soul mate." It sounds romantic—so he can get away with it—but it's also a perfect cop-out.

He isn't feeling many social pressures to marry. No longer are the same pressures exerted from religious institutions, employers, or society to marry as there were in the past. Men can get ahead sans spouse in this day and age. In fact for the most part, nobody in the corporate world cares if a man is single or involved as long as he makes money and does his job. And while some religions still advocate marriage as the ultimate proclamation of love, it no longer seems an absolute necessity in order to be considered devout. So if no one cares if a guy is married or single, then why should he? Once again, society is giving single men a get-out-of-jail-free card when it comes to marriage. The only person who might still be able to exert pressure is his mother, but even that's iffy. As a result, the vulnera-phobic man can cruise along in his unwed state for years without it significantly affecting other areas of his life.

He's reluctant to marry a woman who already has children. The desire to sire is instinctive. The desire to be a father to some other guy's kids? Not so natural. It's sudden responsibility without the pleasure of getting there. For a single mother, it can be a difficult situation if she gets involved with a vulnera-phobic man. She is looking for a partner; he sees her as a woman with whom he can safely get involved because if it gets too serious for his comfort level, her children give him a built-in escape clause.

He wants to own a house before taking a wife. Sure, and you'd like a Porsche before you get a husband but that doesn't stop you. Using the acquisition of tangibles is certainly an easy excuse for the vulnera-phobic man to latch onto because there's no definite end. He might get the house but then want a bigger house, or a boat, or a retirement fund, or whatever. While some degree of financial stability is certainly going to make a man feel more worthy of being a provider, it seems to be in conflict with the previously discussed idea that a single man is afraid a woman will threaten his billfold. Many a couple has made it on love and a desire to be together. Basic needs aside . . . we think this one is plain silly.

He wants to enjoy single life as long as he can. He figures he can stay the bachelor version of Peter Pan forever. The thing is, living out this male fantasy can actually prevent a single guy from maturing. Instead of looking at a woman as a potential partner and learning to respect the opposite sex, this type of vulnera-phobic male tends to view females as conquests, just another notch on his bedpost. By objectifying women, he's able to fully protect his sense of masculinity (guarded emotions and all).

The thing to keep in mind with each entry in this list is how they affect your ability to find a forever man today (not tomorrow when he decides he might be willing to face the emotional insecurities that being in a committed relationship entails). You can look at each of the previous reasons young men cited for not marrying and see them for what they are—excuses. But how can you find a man who can be encouraged to ditch the excuses? We'll show you.

How to Identify the Marrying Kind

So, in the good news department, while the National Marriage Project studies confirm that there are a myriad of reasons why a man might be commitment-phobic, they also found that most men ultimately end up becoming the marrying kind. Among all men surveyed, those from traditional, religiously observant family backgrounds were more likely to be married, to seek marriage, and to have positive views of marriage, women, and children than young males from non-traditional and nonreligious family backgrounds. That said, in the twenty-five- to thirty-four-year-old age bracket, two out of ten unmarried men claimed to be personally averse to tying the knot and expressed negative views about marriage, women, and children. The big question then becomes, how can you recognize the other eight unmarried men who aren't marriage-shy?

Check out the following stats to decide if you've got a committed hunk or a potential runaway groom.

81 percent of married men surveyed agreed with the statement that they decided to get married because it was the right time in their life to settle down. The median age for men to first marry is now twenty-seven (adding another year or two for college-educated men)—a number that is at least four years older than related stats from the 1970s. Researchers believe this has to do with lengthier educational pursuits, career agendas, and a lack of societal pressure to marry at an earlier age. The important thing to remember here, however, is that most men still want to see marriage as a decision they make themselves, when it fits their timeline.

Only 15 percent of married men agreed that they were pressured by their wife to marry at an earlier age than they were ready. What should you take out of this stat? That the men that *did* marry (the majority) were not the ones that felt coerced into it In other words, forcing the issue might get you a ring on your finger, but will it actually get you a man who walks down the aisle or someone who remains faithful to you? In that scenario the truth is that the odds are against you. Keep this in mind the next time you're tempted to start pushing your boyfriend for more. Threats or undue pressure are not the best route to "I do." There are more effective, subtle ways of getting your guy to step up to the plate, which we'll discuss later on.

35 percent of married men disagreed that they got married primarily because they were ready to have children. This goes back to the difference between the female and male biological clock. Throw out the *baby* word too soon and you might see your man run in the opposite direction. A better bet, show your nurturing side. Why? Because although men don't necessarily want to talk about having babies right now, they do tend to consider whether a woman they're dating might be a good choice for bearing their children sometime down the road. In fact, 75 percent of married men in the twenty-five- to thirty-four-year-old age bracket agreed that when choosing a wife, they specifically looked for someone who would also be a good mother.

53 percent of unmarried men who say their fathers were involved in their upbringing claim they're "ready to marry." Though it's not an absolute predictor, studies show that individuals with strong family ties and parental involvement may be less hesitant to jump into a matrimonial situation. So, while the saying goes, "Love him, love his family," the more appropriate saying for this I-seek-commitment situation is "If he loves his family, you can feel safer about loving him."

55 percent of unmarried men who regularly attend religious services say they'd be ready to marry tomorrow if the right person came along. Studies indicate that a man with a religious belief system, whatever denomination it may be, is more likely to be pro-marriage and pro-family. That doesn't mean a man has to be religious in order to commit, but it relates to the point again that if a man has been surrounded with positive messages about commitment while growing up, then he will also be more willing to consider it as a potential asset in his own life.

40 percent of unmarried men studied claim they wouldn't want to get married until they could afford a nice wedding. What does this mean to you? Well, if you're more interested in the wedding, you'll just have to wait until his finances are in order (and who knows when that might be). We think it would be more useful to decide if this is the man you want. Perhaps calming your beau's fears that you don't need him to provide a fairy-tale wedding might actually get you closer to commitment. The thing to realize is that men think of commitment in tangible terms, without taking into account the other qualities that are truly the more important part of the equation.

With the ideas of this chapter in mind, you can begin to see what leads a man toward commitment and what might lead him astray. Now it's time to figure out if you want your man to commit, and what you can do to subtly help move things along if your answer is "yes." Every individual relationship is different, but once you know the pieces of your puzzle, it'll be easier to discern if you're part of a couple with real lasting potential, or if you should consider cutting your losses now and start looking for someone who can make you happy in the way that you desire.

THE CÔMMITMENT-READY MAN ... Commits when he is ready, not when he is forced. It is important to discern how your man defines commitment and see if you share his definition and timeline. If not, you may be waiting a long, long while for him to become yours forever.

COMMITMENT
and Sex

*C*ongratulations! You're getting some. And so is he. Chances are you're both thrilled. Because seriously, who doesn't enjoy sex? But once the postcoital buzz wears off, well *vive la* difference. Men are likely thinking, *Wow, that was awesome! Let's do it again!* Women? Something more along these lines: *Wow, that was awesome! If we keep doing this, we're going to be together forever.* Not so fast.

While one would hope that two people in a between-the-sheets relationship are at least committed to sexual safety, having regular sex with each other does not necessarily mean they are committed in the forever sense of the word. Yet too many women assume that when they sleep with a man, it's moving in a more serious direction. Sadly for these women, they've missed an important point. For many men sex is nothing more than just sex. It's a feel-good moment in time, not a pledge of their heart, fidelity, or even another date.

That said, we agree that great sex is an important part of a committed relationship. A couple needs to have sexual chemistry in order for things to last. And most people in this day and age would agree it's better to find out if that sizzle is there way before walking down the aisle. But notice we said *part* of a committed relationship. There is so much more a good relationship offers, and you deserve all of that and more. To get your just rewards, however, you need to learn to recognize the signs of a relationship based solely on sex (which will likely end before commitment) and one that has a chance for long-term survival.

Coitus Compartmentalization

To better understand the male psyche when it comes to sex, you need to understand one thing: Men are able to separate lust and love. In fact, for them, these two emotions can fall into completely different categories. Don't worry though, just because men are *able* to separate the two doesn't mean they're *always* separate. Many a man has fallen in love with the object of his desire, and conversely discovered intense lust for the woman he loves. But the important thing to note is that men *can* keep the two disconnected.

Most women, on the other hand, don't learn to delineate between the physical and mental aspects of sex. To them, sexual relations are about more than an eventual orgasm (though the latter is always nice if it happens). But for women, sex also includes trust, connection, romance, passion, adoration, and, yes, feelings of love. So, while a good, no-strings-attached romp is sometimes just the ticket, most of the time, a woman is only open to that kind of sex if she's had her other emotional needs fulfilled as well. For that reason, it is exceedingly difficult for a woman to understand that her man might just be boinking sans feelings.

Unfortunately, however, that is exactly what could be happening. When it comes to sex, there is no ignoring the fact that a man and woman may both enjoy the interaction but for entirely different reasons. For a woman, a sexual encounter usually goes back to her wanting and needing to feel secure. She loves the idea of being held, touched, and made to feel adored. She wants to know that a man thinks she's simultaneously wonderful and sexy-as-hell. And it's okay if she feels a little vulnerable in the process, as long as the man she's with makes love to her, which for a woman includes a connection that transcends the body. In the process of having sex, if there is any tenderness involved (such as passionate kissing and touching in addition to just doing the deed), she will feel like the man is into her as well as in her.

Even if a man is successful at making a woman feel special for sleeping with him, he may still be capable of disconnecting his emotions from his sexual behavior. Why are men better at compartmentalizing these feelings? Well, even though it sounds trite, they really are wired differently. Remember, hormones play a part in the brain's function. And testosterone definitely can do a number on the male psyche. Men have a biological urge to procreate that is independent of their need for love and security. Don't think for a moment, however, that we're saying a man can use that as an excuse. If a guy you're dating ever says, "I have a high testosterone level that rules my actions so don't take it personally if I hit on other women—it's my hormones talking," you seriously have our permission to slap him silly. Just because he is a man doesn't mean he gets to act like a Neanderthal. That said, it is important to recognize that his urge-to-merge may sometimes override rational male thought.

Separate from Birth

Hormones notwithstanding, it also pays to revisit the idea that men are socialized differently than women. Men spend their whole lives showing that they're strong and stoic. And this begins at a very young age. Consider that most often the primary caregiver for a child is a woman. Therefore, a little girl will easily identify with this role model. She wants to be like her, be friends with her, behave like her, and please her.

A little boy, however, recognizes the difference between he and his female caregiver. He somehow gets a message, whether innate or societal, that he's not supposed to be like her. He's supposed to be masculine. So early on in his development he will start trying to separate from his opposite (which is usually "Mom," "Grandma," or "Nanny"). He strives to be independent; he heads into the men's room alone; he wants to take care of things himself, like a grownup. Why is this? Practically from birth, boys are bombarded with messages about how they need to "be a man"—thanks to the media, society, and other children.

So, the point here is that boys start to try to separate from women early on whereas girls try to bond. It's not surprising then to learn that from a psychological standpoint, men tend to have a lifelong struggle with connection and women struggle with separation. The fact that men can learn to separate their important relationships into compartments, however, may explain a great deal.

The Friendship Dynamic

To get a clearer picture of this as it relates to you and your relationship with your man, let's first consider friendships. While women don't tend to compartmentalize their gal pals (a woman's friend is a friend in all areas—across the board), most of the time men approach their platonic friendships as side-by-side relationships, which means they tend to do certain things together. Each guy friend will likely have a specific place in a male's friendship schematic. For example, a man might have his golf buddy, his tennis buddy, his drinking buddy, his work buddy, and so on. And it's probable that they may not bond outside of that arena.

Notice, however, that these tidy little buddy categories do a terrific job of letting a guy have his posse without requiring that he open up or share his emotions with any of them. And this detached sort of attachment allows a man to feel like he has friends who've "got his back"—guy-talk for taking care of each other—without feeling any threat to his masculinity . . . or theirs. In fact, this sort of male friend behavior enhances the idea that relationships and emotions aren't necessarily connected.

When men get involved with women, however, they are faced with the prospect of having to adjust to the female definition of what being a "friend" entails (at least when it comes to relating to her). Since friendship is an all-inclusive endeavor for women, they expect that their partner/lover will also turn out to be their confidant/best friend. And because women are used to sharing everything with their friends—and vice versa—they assume it should be no different with their significant other. However, for a man, this is vulnerability in its worst incarnation. Why? Well, in his mind it makes no sense to willingly divulge his perceived shortcomings to anyone, let alone the woman he's supposed to be impressing. A woman, on the other hand, probably thinks that sharing one's deepest thoughts, feelings, and emotions is indicative of closeness and trust. Basically, this boils down to the idea that while most men want a woman in their lives, the idea of having to open up to her and "be close" scares them to death. So, a man tries to convince himself that those warm feelings he gets during sex fall into a category that has nothing to do with his potential out-of-bed feelings toward her. If he keeps them in separate categories, then he's safe . . . right?

Well, maybe in his own mind, but we're unconvinced. He may not be as safe as he would be just throwing up a huge wall to protect himself from a perceived threat to his manhood. But we also have another theory. Though we don't have scientific proof, it's probably not far off base to surmise that some apparently vulnera-phobic men may actually be more of the sensitive type themselves but worry that their masculinity is at risk when they let their emotions creep into the bedroom. In other words, they are afraid that if they allow themselves to feel connected while having sex, their emotions will collide with their hormones and trick them into getting closer to a female than they feel comfortable. For that reason, vulnera-phobes might distance themselves during sex because it scares them to realize they may actually care for the woman with whom they're having intercourse. And god forbid that should happen! If he cares about her, he's no longer in control and, well, you can see how a guy questioning his vulnerability in the bedroom would find that frightening.

Bottom line: Women tend to think in terms of mind/body/soul being inextricably linked. Men, however, can separate mind from body from soul. Sure it's great when they all intersect, but . . . if they don't, he knows he can still have great sex without it. So now that we've got that established, how does sex factor into the commitment conundrum?

Sex and the Single Guy

It really shouldn't come as a surprise when we tell you that the number one reason men are in no hurry to marry today is that sex has become easier to get without having to take that commitment step. What makes matters worse is that this allows single men to successfully avoid their own feelings of vulnerability—the issue that underlies all the others. As long as they're still getting some, men are able to convince themselves that things are just fine. But if a woman they've been having sex with starts to push for more, they know they can avoid any state of unease they might feel by bailing and finding another willing bedmate.

Meanwhile women struggle with the reality of their fertility. Women interested in a family want and need commitment more than men do. They feel they have to settle down sooner rather than later, while men can say, "I've got plenty of time to settle down." This predicament can lead women to compromise their better judgment, often holding onto a relationship longer than might be prudent. But how can a woman know when it's time to throw in the towel and when she should hang in there? Which relationships are classic single-guy sexcapades and which ones might actually stand a chance of turning into something long term? You need to keep a keen eye in order to understand which is which.

....

He Loves Me, He Loves Me Not?

Consider Jeff and Marjorie. At age 31, Jeff is well on his way to supervising the manufacturing division of a large tech company, and Marjorie at 33 has just had her first art exhibition. They have been dating for a year or so. He says he loves her—most often, right before they have sex, sometimes right after. She loves him and tells him regularly, in bed and out. When she says, "I love you," randomly outside the bedroom, he replies, "I don't want to lose you." She can't imagine her life without him, so she believes he is reciprocating her love. But pay attention to the

43

word choice and the timing on his part. He's still protecting his masculinity by refusing to allow himself to sound vulnerable.

That said, both Jeff and Marjorie agree that the sex is great. For most of their relationship, Marjorie has classified Jeff's behavior as attentive and very romantic. Accordingly, she believes this is a sign that he is into her as more than just a sexual plaything. What she may not know, however, is that these behaviors are also indicative of a sexually aroused man, not necessarily one deeply in love. How so? Well, most single men realize that a woman won't usually just jump into bed without some kind of wooing—and Jeff has his MO down to a science.

In truth, however, Marjorie is now beginning to notice that Jeff is attentive and very romantic only when he's horny. Marjorie has mixed feelings about this. She loves that he showers her with gifts and dinners out, but she's noticed it increases when he wants sex. Still, she revels in feeling attractive and desired. When her previous lover lost interest in her, her self-esteem plummeted. She wondered if she'd lost her sex appeal. Jeff's attention restored her sexual confidence.

On the other hand, she's starting to feel used by Jeff. She's having sex when she really isn't in the mood, just to please him—and not just occasionally, but frequently. Secretly she worries he will leave her if she isn't responsive to his needs.

One day she says to Jeff: "Honey, I think we should get married." He seems to have trouble catching his breath and chokes out, "I'm not ready yet!" What gives?

Sadly for Marjorie, as with other women in similar situations, Jeff shows all the signs of being out for sex only—not love and marriage. This relationship is far from the dream situation most women envision. It is no surprise that eventually Marjorie realizes she's feeling less and less like Jeff's girlfriend and more and more like his possession. He knows what to do to keep her hooked—and therefore available for his sexual gratification—but he isn't giving her the real support and love that she needs. She's ready for a forever commitment; he's only committed to her body.

....

So what's a woman to do? Stop having sex completely? Revert to the days of no premarital sex? No—we don't think you have to be *that* extreme. But if commitment and marriage are your goal, then it would be smart for you to learn the signs that will help you determine when a man is pursuing you for something long term and when a man is really just hoping to have you around for sex.

Spotting the "Sex Only" Signs

When trying to sort out where a man falls on the scale of "Just Sex" versus "Settling Down," how can you know if he's into you as a complete package or into your body and what it can do for his package? To give you a leg up on the situation, we've compiled some clues that will allow you to discern when a guy is seeing you as a convenience instead of a commitment.

He spends more money on you when he's looking to get laid. As we mentioned, most single guys know that they have to give something to get some. But when a guy thinks it's all about the stuff he gives you or the places he takes you, he is likely not looking for a relationship. More probable? He's hoping to buy his way into more sex. Pay particular attention to this clue if you realize that a guy you're seeing starts spending more and more on you, but then always seems to expect a reward (read: *sex*) in exchange for his generosity. Romance doesn't involve getting a credit card limit raised to buy flowers, candy, and diamond "Just Because" necklaces. Presents are wonderful, but not when there is expectation attached to the gift. A man who is looking for more than just sex will recognize this and will not try to give a woman things as a substitute for the support, security, and love she really deserves.

He ogles other women even though he's with you. No doubt if you're dating a guy, there are times when he's affectionate and attentive and all over you. And you love it (as you should). But honestly ask yourself if those times are more often than not followed by sex. Also, what happens when you're out and intercourse is not going to happen anytime soon? Do you notice his eyes wandering to the girls at the next table, the waitress in the too-short skirt, or even the TV where a hot Beyoncé video is playing? It's normal for both of you to occasionally check out the opposite sex. Like the saying goes, you're taken, not dead. Attractive people are eye-catching. But if your man lets his eye wander a little too much when he's with you or even ignores you in order to take a gander at some chick, then the signs are pretty clear he's after booty and you're part of that plan but not likely the end of it.

He only wants to have sex when *he* wants it. And he doesn't really seem to care if you're in the mood, or if you're satisfied during the act. If sex is only viewed as the goal and the woman as only the means to that goal, a sex/emotion separatist will easily forget about the feelings of the woman involved. It may take two to tango, but if you find that the man you're with is all about his pleasure then it's likely he's not thinking of you as someone he cherishes and adores. A man looking for a relationship will understand if you really do have a headache or are exhausted from a rough day at work. Sex is a *part* of a real relationship, not all of it.

He always has an excuse to delay commitment talk. It's his job, his family responsibilities, his student loans, his new dog, his apartment issues, his . . . *whatever*. You get the picture. A man who is not even willing to entertain the idea of the future is one that is not looking for a real relationship. Chatting about what you want in life and your "someday" wishes is an important part of a couple's development. If you are being deprived of that blissful state of duo-dreaming, then it's likely he's only thinking as far as your next sack session, which really doesn't give you much to build a relationship on.

He won't say the L word—even if you've been together for a long time! Every man (and woman, of course) has his own meter for when he's ready to say, "I love you" (and mean it). But if a man you've been exclusively dating for six to eight months can't say it, other than pre- or postcoitus, it's likely he's less in love with you and more in love with the sex.

So, now what happens if you're Marjorie and you've realized that the man you're seeing is all about sex? A lot of women like her will still believe they can make it happen by trying harder and they don't want to hear otherwise. This is especially true if they can point to a potential Mr. Right's romantic behavior as a validation of his feelings instead of what it really is: foreplay.

But let's discuss this further. Let's say she does decide to stay with it. What is she hoping for? The chance that he will change his mind? That one day he'll wake up and realize she's the one? Whatever she's wishing for, it probably won't happen. If Jeff's biological clock isn't telling him it's time to commit, there's no point in her pushing him. Marjorie can make the mistake of giving him an ultimatum (as many women do), making promises about how great she'll be to him, and even eventually snag him, but if he's not ready, chances are he'll only end up resenting her for it, or worse—cheating or leaving.

As soon as there's the first bump in the road, he'll turn on her and say, "See, I knew I wasn't ready, but you pressured me."

Men tend to be, by nature, the pursuers, aggressors, and hunters. You would not expect a fish to jump out of the water and start walking on land, so don't expect a man to stop being a man. If Jeff wanted a future with Marjorie, he would want to be with her even when sex wasn't on his mind. But if he's only in it for the pursuit, then Jeff's only going to want to be with her when he's hunting for sex. Women will make up excuses for this type of male action—not calling, keeping dates, or making plans on his own. They think they have to put in the effort for him in order for the relationship to function. But the truth is: Nothing will get in a man's way if he really wants to be with a woman.

If Jeff feels coerced and eventually concedes to her marriage demands, Marjorie will pay for his concession. Ever hear the phrase, "It will come back to bite you in the butt?" That's exactly what will happen here. Maybe he'll bite her gently by making her feel unsure and question if he really loves her, or have her thinking he would really rather be with someone else. Or the bite could be much more painful. He could leave her for another woman, who's perhaps not even as attractive or successful but one that he chose and pursued and freely committed to—thus boosting his feelings of masculinity while suppressing feelings of vulnera-phobia at the same time.

So, what should Marjorie do about Jeff? Well, she could break up with him and start dating other men. And yes, that could possibly have the side effect of making Jeff realize that he really does love her and was taking her for granted. But making Jeff jealous is not the game she should be playing. If she goes back to dating it should be because she realizes that she still hasn't found a man who shares her desire for marriage and a family, or at least one who is on her timeline for those things.

Conversely, she could stick it out for a while longer and see if anything changes. But she has to make one pivotal change herself: She has to agree that she will only have sex when she feels like it. No more having sex to "keep her man." His reaction to her self-commitment will help give her the knowledge she needs to ultimately decide if she should stay, or if she should go.

Vulnerability and Sex

When a man is on top of his game sexually, he's on top of the world. Why? It's a control thing. When he's calling the shots and feeling *oh-my-god* good, that nerve-wracking state of vulnerability he tries desperately to avoid takes a backseat for a while. Sex becomes a euphoric drug, and accordingly he wants more of it. Sounds a little addicting, doesn't it?

Well, that may be exactly what the problem is with the man who distances himself emotionally during sex. In a sense he becomes addicted to the high he gets from being in charge of his body and his emotions. And he watches that energy carry over in his dealings with other men too. If he's getting some regularly, he is suddenly part of the cool crowd, and he trusts that he can hang with the boys on equal footing because he knows he's well hung (or at least using what he's got to his advantage).

One problem for men who play the sex/emotions separation game though, is that they don't realize there are abundant benefits attached to emotionally connected sex. This is primarily because they won't let themselves try it; it's too scary to even consider. However, unless the guy you're with is actually one of the 22 percent of men who falls into the National Marriage Project's "Non-marrying kind" category (a group that routinely mistrusts women, worries about divorce before they're even hitched, and thinks single men have better sex lives than married men), you may be able to introduce the idea of true intimacy—emotionally connected sex—into your bedroom relationship.

Though we're not claiming that you can make a vulnera-phobic guy suddenly want to commit to you by doing these things, you can certainly test the waters to see if he might be able to handle a more involved relationship by way of the bedroom. At the very least, introducing some emotional intimacy during and after sex will allow you to see if there is even a remote possibility of emotional commitment from him now or in the future. If not, it might be better to cut bait and look for another fish in the sea.

Here are some ways to make your sex sessions emotionally charged:

Make eye contact during sex. It's much easier for a man to disconnect the sexual act from the woman he's with if he's not focused on her. By getting him to lock eyes with you during intercourse, you are effectively forcing him to recognize that the body underneath (or above) his is a living, breathing, feeling person. Whether he recognizes this or the message seeps in subconsciously, working to make your man *see* that you are part of his sexual experience (not just some random chick he's banging) can allow him to realize that part of why he feels so good is not just that he's having sex, but that he's having sex specifically with *you*.

Kiss, kiss, kiss. Mouth to mouth is intimate. It triggers an immediate emotional connection. If he's just thrusting and not trusting, keep your man kissing you during sex. You can even combine the previous tip and make him kiss you with his eyes open! The effect is undoubtedly jarring for the man who has been disconnecting during sex, but it will keep him rooted in the present and not mentally playing out some sexual fantasy that doesn't involve you.

Give him positive reinforcement. During the act let him know how amazing he's making you feel and how incredible you think he looks, acts, kisses, or any other compliment you can think of. He'll start to feel good not just about the act of sex, but he'll realize that he likes having sex with *you* because you make him more masculine and less vulnerable.

Try a little after-play. Instead of letting him jump up right after sex, ask him to hold you for a while. He may resist because cuddling after sex is a totally vulnerable time for him (especially when he's just reached a peak that can flood his body with hormonal and emotional aftershocks). He may not trust himself or what might come out of his mouth après sex. But by getting him used to the idea of being with you at a time when he's feeling a little less like a lion, you can also ease him into the idea that while he doesn't want to appear vulnerable in life, it is okay for him to be vulnerable and close to you for ten minutes after sex. You can just spoon quietly, or you can use that time to talk. Whatever you do, however, resist the urge to say, "What are you thinking?" That will probably induce panic. What you can do is reinforce how lovely the experience of being together is for you and how connected it makes you feel. In time, he might start to realize that he feels the same way.

All of the previous steps to fostering a sexual *and* emotional connection in the bedroom will help guys realize that a session of lovemaking is much more enjoyable and arousing than just seeking a quick orgasm. This is an important lesson for single men to learn because precommitment many of them are looking at marriage as the end of their sex life. What they need to recognize, however, is that they may actually enjoy their sex life more when there is trust and connection with a woman that they care about. In fact, according to the National Marriage Project, 73 percent of the married men surveyed claimed that their sex life was better after they got married. That's a *huge* blow to the single guy's belief that marriage will end his sexual pleasure.

That said, a guy has to be ready to accept that sex is more than just being physical. If a man is not mature enough emotionally and intellectually, there may be nothing you can do to convince him that a relationship is about more than his bedtime rituals. In other words, you can't force a sexually immature man to step up to the plate. If, however, you get a positive response after trying some of the previous tips, you may want to give him a little more time and see if he can discover how fulfilling connected sex can be. (The caveat being that you don't tell him this is what you're doing—men like to think they've made these discoveries by themselves). The question you have to ask yourself is: *How much time am I willing to give him to grow into the man I want him to be?*

And along with that, you'll have to decide where your limits are when it comes to "sharing," which we'll discuss in the next chapter. For most women, they'll give everything they have to the right man, but they want to know that he's theirs and theirs alone in return.

THE COMMITMENT-READY MAN ... Knows that random sex is more readily available to him than ever before in today's society but chooses instead to explore the benefits of emotionally intimate sex. He recognizes that sex is *part* of a relationship, not all of it. And he's mature enough to understand that connected sex can be deeper and more fulfilling than just the physical act.

4

COMMITMENT
Is Exclusivity

Whatever you're ultimately hoping for in a relationship, there is one thing that is usually non-negotiable: Loyalty. It's about knowing that your man is yours and yours alone. And it's not so much born out of jealousy, like in the way men get consumed when they're worried that another man might be moving in on their territory. It's more that women—who by nature are the more giving of the sexes—will gladly share anything with others except when it comes to something that might threaten their sense of security, which as you'll recall is the basis of female commitment.

So, while men may be programmed to spread their seed, women are biologically wired to nest, and to them that usually means with one faithful partner. But while women welcome the idea of being with one person for life as a comforting concept, the majority of yet-to-commit men shudder in panic at the very idea. According to the Rutgers' National Marriage Project, men also have a grave fear of the financial impact of divorce, which increases their hesitancy to commit even further. Having not yet experienced any of the benefits that come from true commitment, single men are working off of what they've seen on television, what their buddies tell them, and what they assume coupling up means—never having sex with another woman!

This suggests that once again a good deal of the commitment conundrum is actually related to the male/female perception of the term. With that in mind, let's take a closer look at what women and men think being exclusive entails.

Gender-Specific Definitions of *Exclusive*

It usually goes like this: girl and boy meet, girl and boy click, girl and boy start dating, girl and boy start having sex, girl and boy find themselves in a relationship, and then things get tricky. Girl thinks, *Wow, this is going great. We're boyfriend and girlfriend now and that means we're exclusive.* Boy thinks frantically, *Wait, how did I get to this point? I dig this chick but does that mean I won't be able to sleep with another woman if I say we're an item? And is she going to expect this to be serious and are we moving too fast and does she think we're exclusive now and . . . ?* Get the picture?

In a woman's ideal world, all the steps toward commitment happen in perfect progression. In fact, most think relationships should go from meeting to madly in love to marriage—an order befitting those childhood fairy tales women still want to believe can come true. Unfortunately getting to happily ever after is usually a little bumpier. Especially when you throw your potential Prince Charming into the mix, who may be amazing and wonderful but completely vulnera-phobic at the same time.

Why is this? Well, when it comes to saying, "You're the one," there are a myriad of little steps that have to be taken on the road to forever, like feeling that his career is in place, his financial outlook is sunny, and, of course, he had ample time to play the field and compromise—dare we say it—his freedom. For women, however, that path is usually quite straightforward. Men, on the other hand, tend to get caught up in a slew of detours along the way. It's sort of like women take the express highway toward commitment and men prefer the scenic route. The trick for women, however, is learning to discern which detours are dead ends and which ones are merely deviations from the course.

You can begin to figure out which is which by considering the difference between what men and women perceive exclusivity to mean. Women view exclusivity as emotional and physical monogamy. That is, her man is not having any kind of sex with someone else. It also includes him not having an intimate nonsexual relationship with another woman, unless his girlfriend has given him a pass on the latter because she considers the other woman not to be a threat for whatever reason.

Women also see exclusivity as security. In their mind it means they no longer have to worry about being on the competitive dating market. Once they have a partner, it's like another item has been checked off their female "To Do" list. This accomplishment is a boon to their self-regard, and will also bring about a sense of peace and well-being. Exclusivity means she's succeeded—she's got a match that will be loyal so she can rest easy and take comfort in the idea that she never again has to risk giving her heart to a man who might trample it. Finding a relationship gives her more freedom.

On the flip side, men equate exclusivity with a *loss* of freedom. In most cases, they just assume that agreeing to be with only one woman means the end of their life as they know it; instead of seeing it as the beginning of something wonderful like the majority of women view it. Why else would bachelor parties have that last-night-to-live edge to them? Rather than see committing to one woman as a positive event, men are socialized to believe becoming exclusive means giving something up.

With that in mind, it's no surprise that few guys will lunge at the chance to seal off their romantic options by getting into an exclusive relationship. Accordingly, one major detour on the path to permanence is an overwhelming temptation for men to keep playing the field. Knowing he still has options gives a man the feeling that he's not accountable to any one woman, which serves as the perfect antidote to any vulnera-phobic feelings encountered along the way. Unfortunately, most women are not going to be okay with a guy who wants to eat his cake and have it too!

This intrinsic male aversion to exclusivity also confirms what many women have suspected all along: A significant percentage of men are simply poor candidates for long-term commitment. And no, we're not talking about the guys who can't keep a job, who hang around off-track betting offices all day, or whose closest companion is a beer can. We are talking about the ones who just can't seem to keep it in their pants.

Men who feel compelled to continue playing the field are most likely going to fall into the vulnera-phobic category. These smooth talkers know how to work the game to keep their options open while keeping their vulnerability at bay. But what's lacking in their dating prowess is maturity. The good news is that eventually some of them may grow up and realize that hopping from bed to bed is unfulfilling. Unfortunately, many of them may not.

In fact, 20 percent of single men in the twenty-five- to thirty-four-year-old category admit they are "personally averse to marriage." That's one in five! And sadly—especially for the commitment-minded women out there—it's a respectable chunk of available males.

Even more disturbing for single women, many of these guys may be out there dating. They know the drill and they know how to charm the pants off a woman—they just don't know how to commit to one. Your only defense is to learn the telltale signs of the man who may act as if you're his main dish, but who sees nothing wrong with having a few blond, brunette, or redhead side dishes. Here are ten important clues that your guy may be ordering up something extra:

1. His eyes start to wander when you're around other women—not occasionally and casually, but obsessively and intensively.
2. He's has periods of time where he doesn't answer his cell and reasons for being out-of-touch that create suspicion.
3. He explains that all the girls he hangs out with are just old friends. And, when an ex is going through a hard time, he runs to her aid saying he would feel guilty not helping her out.
4. He's still got his old flames' phone numbers and e-mail addresses actively listed in his BlackBerry.
5. You're on birth control and don't use condoms with him—but you've noticed a stash of condoms at his place.
6. He overtly flirts with every attractive woman he meets and tells you he's just being friendly.
7. You've caught him in small lies and have begun to wonder what else he's lying about.
8. His cell phone rings late at night, but he won't take the calls if you're around.

9. You've discovered he's cruising the personals online and in the newspaper.
10. You search and find he has a profile posted on an online dating site and when you call him out, he says he forgot it was still posted.

If you notice any one of these traits, it's not an encouraging sign. However, put two or more together and there is definitely an egregious violation of good boyfriend behavior going on. If he's not a full-blown vulnera-phobic cad, then he's at least got some of the symptoms and you may be in for heartbreak if you try to make this man commit before he matures. Why? Try as you might, forcing exclusivity on a man who isn't ready does not usually yield favorable results. Men don't like to be pushed into doing anything. They want to believe that it's their choice to be with one woman. Therefore, if the man you're seeing is a total player (i.e., exhibits most of the violations on the previous list), you might have a serious decision to make.

If you're okay with dating a man who cheats on you, that's your prerogative and you can stay in the relationship. However, we're guessing that's not what you're really after—so read on.

The Forever Freakout

Here's a little secret we want to share with you: Most guys actually *want* to be in a committed relationship. However, when they suddenly find themselves close to exclusivity, a little voice starts whispering in their heads and instead of "Commit, commit, commit" all they can hear is "Abort, abort, abort!" The result of this usually leaves the woman shaking her head in utter confusion as her man runs the other way and has a *Forever Freakout*.

What triggers a FF episode? Any number of things. One possibility, of course, is that the woman starts pushing for more. Though many men *do* need a nudge toward commitment, overt demands for exclusivity are more likely to cause a panic than a promise. That is why we keep encouraging you to think subtle when it comes to applying pressure for a more defined relationship. Try to force a guy's hand and your left hand will remain ringless—or, worse yet, you'll get that ring and he'll either make you miserable, or bail—and blame it on you!

Another possible FF trigger is that some other male figure—be it a buddy, his brother, his father, or a coworker—points out the possible perils of exclusivity to him and suddenly, where he was feeling happy and secure with you, he's now doubting his own instincts. As callous and as horrible as it is for any other man to intervene in your future happiness, it happens all the time. As soon as your guy gets a "Don't do it man" message from one of his brethren, his vulnera-phobia gets kicked up a notch again and he starts to go over all the horrible things that might happen to his independence if he takes another step with you.

Finally, television and film certainly don't help the female plight for commitment one bit. Iconic sitcoms like *Cheers* and movies like *Hitch* are responsible for constantly bombarding your guy with messages that say agreeing to be exclusive with you totally shuts off any possibility he *ever* has of being a stud ever again. Though it may not even be what he ultimately wants, just the idea that he will be denied something can make a man uneasy.

Again, men don't like to be told what they can and can't do, or what they can and can't have. He needs to feel some semblance of control in his life or his masculinity is threatened, he starts to feel vulnerable, and thoughts of bailing enter his head.

....

Danny's FF Crisis

To bring this point to life, consider Danny, a twenty-six-year-old accountant in what his girlfriend Nancy assumes is a possibly soon-to-be-engaged relationship. Two peas in a pod, Danny and Nancy have been happily dating for over a year and things have been going great. But all of a sudden, Danny is starting to have a FF. He doesn't want to lose Nancy, but when he considers asking her to marry him the thought of lifelong monogamy sends shivers down his spine. In talking about what's going on in his head, he lowers his voice to a whisper as if what he's divulging is a dangerous truth that only applies to him and must not be repeated:

> I don't know if I can do it. I think I'm programmed, genetically, to want to spread my seed. That's why as soon as I started to contemplate getting engaged, or in other words, when it looked like my screwing-around days were over, I found myself in the street comparing babes to my potential bride-to-be. I caught myself thinking, "That one's got great legs—long and thin. Oh, and that one's got great boobs—they look real, naturally firm. And over there ... that one's got that Angelina Jolie wild look—chiseled features, full lips ...wow!"
>
> But what concerned me even more than my sudden "Nancy versus the rest of the female race" comparisons was that I didn't just think about it. ... I started to push the

boundaries a little! One night I was picking up some groceries and there was this hot blond down one of the aisles. I started following her, thinking of ways to start a conversation. When I glanced behind me there were two other guys following along, probably having the same thoughts! It was so clear we were all struggling to resist temptation and it got me thinking . . . is monogamy really a bad joke? I mean is it irrelevant in this day and age when we're living into our nineties? That's a long time with one woman!

Anyway, I couldn't help myself and pushing back the vision of Nancy that flashed before my eyes, I approached Blondie before the posse behind me stole my opportunity. I left the store feeling like a king after we'd exchanged e-mail addresses. But then I also felt like a jerk. . . . What was I doing?

What *was* Danny doing? Danny was having a classic Forever Freakout. He had all the symptoms: Jitters, doubts, sweats, insane testosterone spikes, inexplicable urges to play-the-field. That's because he was imagining a permanent end to his life as a swinging single and all the stuff that goes with that title—partying with the guys, flavor-of-the-month girls, no accountability. Never mind that he was secretly getting tired of hangovers and meaningless encounters. In the face of exclusivity talk, all a vulnera-phobic male can think about is what he'll be giving up. It's a craziness that sets in when a guy realizes he's slipping closer to commitment.

. . . .

One thing you need to recognize is that with some guys a FF may only be a temporary condition, but with others it could be a permanent affliction. The key is to sort out which version you're dealing with. In other words, just because your guy starts freaking out doesn't mean it's time to formulate an exit strategy. However, it may suggest a need to take a closer look at what's going on in your relationship because that will give you the real clues as to whether or not commitment is in the cards.

She Works Hard for Monogamy

Here's a simple fact: Too many women are working too hard to make their relationships work. You argue, *Of course they are—all relationships are work.* Yes, we agree with you. The problem is that unfortunately all too often the relationships women are desperately shoring up don't have a chance. It may be that the guy is emotionally unavailable. Or perhaps he doesn't choose to reciprocate the love of this particular woman. He likes her, he likes having sex with her—but a future with her is just not what he wants. Or maybe he's stuck in a vulnera-phobic quagmire and doesn't have the maturity to slosh his way out.

Whatever the case, a woman can kill herself to try and make a dead-end relationship work because she wants it so badly, but it won't matter if he's not going to participate in it. A relationship is a two-way street; you both have to be in it and you both have to want it. Sadly, however, many women get desperate—be it as a result of their ticking clock or even just their inherent need for security—and they decide: "Well, maybe the shoe doesn't fit perfectly, but if I jam my foot in it might just fit and won't hurt me or give me blisters." *Seriously?* There is no reason to stick with someone who isn't the right fit. In other words, don't try to force yourself into something just because it's in style. Your friends may be coupling up, but that doesn't mean you have to follow the trend if you haven't yet found the perfect pairing.

The underlying problem here is that if you find yourself doing all the work in the relationship, you're settling. Is that really what you want? Is that how you wish to spend the rest of your life? You may be able to deal with it now but think ahead. What happens down the road after years of you working to cement the relationship? Years of giving, giving, giving. Are you truly going to be happy just because you have a commitment? Doubtful.

But many women in this situation don't practice foreshadowing. They are just thinking of holding together their relationship now. To compensate for their guy's emotional and sometimes physical unavailability many women do all or most of the work to maintain a semblance of connection. This may mask the situation for a while, but not forever. When they've stopped doing all that work, they notice there is no relationship, or not enough of one to sustain their emotional needs.

Doing all the labor in a relationship is not loving, giving, or caring. It is self-defeating and relationship-defeating. And, it's not really motivated by altruism. Why then will a woman choose to assume all the emotional connection efforts? Well, she may convince herself that she's doing it for him, but in reality she's doing all the work because she wants the relationship so badly. To fulfill her fantasy, she creates the illusion of a relationship when in fact there may be no relationship. That enables her guy to neglect his share. Ultimately, however, she'll realize he's not meeting her needs and will feel victimized. To be fair, she's created the victim role for herself. He didn't impose it upon her.

Her behavior, however, has allowed something to develop that isn't authentic. Her guy thinks this is a great relationship because he's getting all the benefits without having to put in any effort. And by allowing things to progress in this manner, the woman has not encouraged her man to want or need to commit at all. She's actually perpetuating his vulnera-phobic behaviors by not requiring that he give her any emotional support. So he feels safe that he's not getting too close and this status quo could go on indefinitely as far as he's concerned.

Although what's more likely to happen is that one day she'll wake up and think, *Hey, what am I getting out of this relationship?* At that point, she'll start to push for more closeness or exclusivity in order to alleviate her own sense of being taken for granted. Her guy will most likely think she's become too demanding rather than actually respond to her legitimate wants. And this problem that arises from her sudden realization will cause an extreme amount of distress, as it does not fit the precedent that she set early on in their relational interactions.

Keep in mind that in our best relationships, we all have temporary periods where one person puts in more than the other. This is normal. But as a permanent way of participating in relationships, the woman-as-worker-bee pattern leaves too many women feeling tired, worn out, needy, and angry. Eventually that repressed anger may also be expressed in lack of sexual desire.

Okay, we now know what you're thinking: *Everybody who watches* Oprah *knows that in most cases it's women who do more of the relationship tending.* The difference is that is in an *established* relationship. When a relationship is developing and is not fully committed, the woman can't carry that load. If she does, she's stifling the newly developing relationship and misrepresenting what she really wants.

The important thing to take away from this discussion in regard to your own relationship is that you should do a reasonable amount of work, but don't do *all* the work. Let the relationship find a balance and you'll be setting yourself up for a stronger future.

Exclusivity and Vulnerability

The underlying question women ask when it comes to exclusivity is: Why would a man who is seemingly in a good relationship suddenly feel the need to screw around and mess things up?

Well, for starters, some of these men are great actors. They might've pretended to be the exclusive type (knowing full well they weren't) in order to get what they wanted for a while. These are the true players and the type of guy that you should dump immediately. They're using you for sex and their own gratification only. But then there are the Danny-types out there.

....

Nancy's FF Crisis

Danny really loves Nancy. Danny could even see a future with Nancy. Danny was on the verge of proposing to Nancy. So what happened?

Well, one really good possibility is that Danny started to feel vulnerable. He realized that in getting closer and closer to Nancy, he was somehow losing sight of himself. However, his panic had absolutely nothing to do with Nancy.

Unfortunately for Nancy, she found out about Danny's exchange with the blond from the supermarket by scanning his e-mail. (Danny was unaware that she had his password and periodically snooped out of curiosity.) The result was her own FF.

I know I shouldn't be snooping. But that's not the point. I did and I'm freaking. The point is that I've been dating Danny for over a year now and the e-mail that I read seems to confirm my worst fears. Lately we have been spending less quality time together. It seems like I usually just go over to his apartment for sex. He's also been a little moody and complains about not having as many buddies as he would like. And as recently as a couple of months ago we were talking engagement. Now he hardly ever mentions our future.

I recently asked him where he saw us in a few years and all he could say was, "I've been so panicky about my job, I haven't been focusing on that." Then he changed the subject and got very nervous and fidgety. He is two years younger than I am—I'm twenty-eight, he's twenty-six—so he might feel he has lots of time before committing. I'm at a point where I don't want to be in a relationship where someone is just using me. Been there, done that.

I need to figure out if this is just a temporary condition that will pass, or if marriage is completely out of the picture. I want a more defined relationship—like I thought we were coming to a couple of months back. I'm scared if I don't do something to take us to the next step, we'll just continue like we have. After all, Danny's a guy. He's got time. If I want a family, and I do, my time will slip away.

Okay, yes, Nancy does have every right to freak out because the signs were definitely incriminating. And she's also right to worry that she and Danny might not be on the same page as far as what exclusivity means. However, what Nancy doesn't know, and what Danny was probably not even consciously aware of, is that often men facing the prospect of exclusivity will increase behaviors that help weaken their feelings of intimacy. Danny was likely flirting with other women and pushing his boundaries in an attempt to dilute the intensity he was feeling in his relationship with Nancy. It was a subconscious effort to regain control of his feelings.

. . . .

Diluting intimacy is something many men find themselves doing when they think a relationship is getting too serious. By acquiring another option or two on the side, it allows them to lessen the magnitude of their primary relationship and the resultant pressure. When a man starts to feel panic about exclusivity, a good deal of that unease probably stems from many of the things that we have discussed already in this chapter, as well as his feelings of losing control. Remember, men don't like to think they are not in charge of their own emotions. It is a very rare man that recognizes his wandering eye may be the result of his own vulnerability—and those that do are likely not the ones straying.

But this doesn't mean that a man who starts to look elsewhere is plotting his escape from the relationship. In fact, if given time to make peace with the idea, he may find that exclusivity is actually what he was craving—he just didn't know for sure yet. How can a woman tell the difference though? What determines if a man has a philandering soul or is just in the midst of a commitment meltdown?

To help figure out where in the commitment process your relationship falls, it's important to discover the answers to the following questions.

Are you and your partner ultimately looking for the same kind of commitment? Remember, commitment-phobes aside, some men may not actually be looking for a relationship that leads to marriage. But they might be okay with a committed long-term relationship, like the one Goldie Hawn and Kurt Russell have enjoyed. If the idea of marriage is important to you, however, then you need to know how he feels about this issue. And if he's not pro-marriage, you need to honestly ask yourself if you can live with another kind of arrangement. If not, this may be a deal-breaker.

Do you and your man define exclusivity the same way? This can be a very gray area when it comes to relationships. Bill Clinton's separation of oral sex from "sexual relations" is just one example of how men can rationalize their way out of all kinds of sexual behavior. While that kind of thinking isn't completely limited to men, it is much more common for them to bend the parameters of exclusivity with things like "She didn't mean anything to me" or "It was a guy thing." Before you can truly be together for the long term, you need to make sure you both have the same definition of exclusivity. If your views are divergent, chances are your relationship will take a nosedive at some point because of poorly communicated rules of conduct.

Have you explicitly discussed exclusivity, or are you working under an assumption? If you and your man have not had a direct chat about exclusivity, then you may not be exclusive. This is one of those things that *must* be discussed. Very frequently people move from a multiple-dating scenario into what seems like a boyfriend/girlfriend relationship without ever having a conversation about it. Sometimes this is just a function of time, which has a way of establishing that kind of connection. But, unless you two have actually talked about not dating other people, you can't be 100 percent sure of what he's thinking, and vice versa. This isn't just for way down the road. You need to determine where you are right now in your relationship to have an idea of where you are heading.

Is there any healthy jealousy happening in your relationship? We're not talking about irrational jealousy—like you're mad that he buys his assistant a gift after she stayed up all night without him to finish a project. That's just nutty. But, if you find yourself feeling a healthy sense of envy when you hear about his ex-girlfriend sending him an e-mail or when he mentions that one of the women at work has a crush on him, then that's a sign you're seeing this relationship as something you want to protect.

Using this same principle, you can gauge his emotional attachment to you by the level of rational jealousy he exhibits when discussing your straight male friends. Chances are that if he's got designs on keeping you in his life for a while, he's going to exhibit some chest-puffing behavior. A commitment-minded man will probably assume that any other straight guy who gets close to you also secretly wants to have sex with you. A good guy will still let you have your male friends, but asking if he gets a little jealous about them can help you determine his investment in your relationship. If his vulnerability shows, chances are he has even more intense emotions for you than he's letting on!

Once you've determined that he's more than a high-flight-risk kind of guy, you can start to work on easing his vulnerability by opening him up to the idea of exclusivity as you see fit.

It's All or Nothing Baby!

The trick to making your man comfortable with the idea of exclusivity is to institute conversations and actions that not only assure your man he needn't give up his independence by being with you, but also let him think that it was *his* idea to agree to exclusivity. As we've discussed, coercion rarely works. And even if it does, it can come back to haunt you.

....

Danny's FF Crisis Subdued

In the case of Danny and Nancy, when Nancy finally called him out on his inappropriate behavior, the riff between them was almost too much to surmount. Initially Danny was completely put off by the fact that Nancy had been snooping on him. But then a funny thing happened. Their conversations about his panic led him to realize just how much Nancy meant to him. And the fact that he could be honest with her and she could listen without killing him for contacting the blond gave him the confidence to realize he would be okay agreeing to a monogamous existence. When he understood that his actions were potentially endangering something of great importance to him, his fears and feelings of vulnerability subsided.

As Danny put it:

I almost bailed. I'm not a hard-sell guy. If Nancy had pushed me, it would probably have ended with me being pushed in the wrong direction. But Nancy wasn't sucked in by the undertow of my freak-out wave; she rode out the storm, which is why she enjoys the calm we now share. She somehow knew—as all women should know—it's during that panic period that a man comes to grips with the fact that he can survive the long, monogamous journey ahead—or that he can't. And, I think I speak for a lot of guys when I say that pushing him in one way or another is not the thing to do. It's gonna come back and bite you, if not right away than later.

So now we are really together—as a committed team. And I am happy about it because I feel it was my decision, made without coercion. Yeah, Nan and I have had our ups and downs, of course, but nothing quite as rocky as my commitment-to-romance jitters.

Fortunately for her relationship's survival, Nancy asked herself some tough questions, read her man right, and knew that it was worth hanging in there. And Danny proved that he was not the completely marriage-phobic type but rather a man in the midst of an all-too-common temporary FF episode.

....

If you're looking for that kind of Danny/Nancy happy ending in your own relationship, however, you might consider trying a couple little tests to determine whether he is ready to consider exclusivity.

Expose him to other exclusive couples that are happy. Arrange a dinner date with two of your friends who have just moved in together, bring him to your cousin's engagement party, or have him escort you to a wedding. Any of these occasions will give you the opportunity to casually say something like, "They look so happy." Then read his response. On the positive side is agreement—some form of affirmation. Of course, there are also signs that he's not sharing your same vision for the future. Look for indications such as sarcasm ("Yeah, but in six months, they'll have put on thirty pounds and stopped having sex"), skepticism ("Really? They seem a little bored"), or sappiness ("Maybe one day..."). These are red flags suggesting that you may need to back off your emotional investment.

Go on a big-ticket shopping excursion. Try taking your man shopping for something you would both enjoy. One possibility is going to a furniture store to look at new couches for his place. If during your trip he tends to be indifferent about finding things to enhance your mutual comfort and instead ends up drifting to the motorcycle dealership across the street (extreme, but you get the point), he's likely not looking for commitment but is rather still caught up in the I'm-single-and-loving-it mentality.

Go out-of-town—without him. Plan a trip to see your parents for a week, or maybe visit your best friend. What happens on his end while you're gone? Does he call you to check in? Text message to say he misses you? E-mail you little notes wishing you a good trip? Or is he suddenly MIA the entire time you're gone? If he's able to slip into out-of-sight, out-of-mind mode when you aren't right in front of him, you are likely dealing with a man who is not keen on exclusivity.

The bottom line here is that when it comes to exclusivity, you have to decide what you can live with right now and what you're hoping for in the future. Then find out where your guy is concerning the subject and take it from there. The most important thing is to gather information so you can make an informed decision before moving toward other commitment steps that might be harder than just a breakup to undo—like cohabitation, which we'll discuss in the next chapter. Making sure you're on the same page when it comes to exclusivity is vital not only for your relationship's survival, but also for your sanity. Do the homework so you'll know how to proceed.

THE COMMITMENT-READY MAN ... Realizes that he can still be independent and exclusive at the same time—in other words, committing to one woman won't end life as he knows it. And, he accepts that intimacy might make him feel vulnerable, but he understands that exclusivity will provide him with a sense of security.

5

COMMITMENT
and Cohabitation

First comes love,
Then comes marriage,
Then comes Jenny with the baby carriage!

*R*emember that childhood chant? Chances are you jumped rope to it at some point during recess, only it was *your* name linked with the baby carriage. You probably didn't know it then, but your little-girl games were subconsciously reinforcing the way you would one day assume a relationship was supposed to happen. Or, at least, how it used to happen. Today it would probably go something more like:

First comes love,

Then comes moving in together,

Then comes . . . we'll see if we're compatible enough to maybe get engaged if he ever gets around to asking and then possibly marry if things work out, and someday have kids.

Seems like things have gotten a *little* more complicated on the playground.

It does indeed seem that there is a new step between love and marriage. According to the Center for Marital and Family Studies at the University of Denver, half of today's marriages are preceded by a period of unmarried cohabitation. But while that stat may sound encouraging to the woman who has just been offered a permanent set of keys, there is also the danger that living together may lead to simply more living together. Studies have shown that one of the main reasons young men today are not committing to a marital union is that they're perfectly happy with the way things are once they're living with their girlfriend.

So, to cohabitate or not to cohabitate . . . that is the question. The answer? Well, it depends. Unfortunately it's not a clear-cut yes or no. Once again, the emotional maturity of the man factors in, as do the reasons for shacking up. However, one thing is for sure, before you say, "Yes, I think we should move in together," some serious thought is in order.

Changing Views on Combining Keys

Once upon a time, the thought of living together before marriage was as unfathomable as, well, having sex without an "I do." But nowadays, couples are frequently opting for one set of keys. So what has the commonality of cohabitation done for the state of commitment? Does sharing a postal address indicate permanence? The problem, once again, is that the answers here are rather nebulous (and likely gender specific), making things a little murky when it comes to the subject of marriage.

When it comes to dating and relating, both men and women who seek an attachment are quite aware of the diversity of serious relationships. There are factors of duration and intensity to consider, but stripped to their basics, committed relationships assume one of three forms: exclusive dating, living together unmarried (LTU), or marriage.

The difference among these forms is in their assumed obligations. Dating exclusively implies sexual exclusivity, living together adds to this an agreement to combine living routines, and marriage has the implication of permanence. Living together unmarried is the midpoint between the least restrictive (exclusive dating) and the most complex (marriage).

The current prevalence of LTUs is a measure of society's changing attitudes. Although cohabitation between the unmarried has always existed in American communities, it was limited to those knowingly living outside of society's conventional boundaries. Today, however, it is an increasingly common practice among those people who fit within society's norms—especially among middle-class couples.

But the prevalence of cohabitation is definitely having an effect on marriage rates. Though many people see living together as an intermediary step between flirting and forever, it may actually be crushing the amount of people tying the knot. In fact, according to the National Marriage Project, the most significant factor contributing to male delay of marriage is the rise of cohabitation.

Why is this? Well, when playing house, men realize they can actually get many of the benefits of marriage—including regular access to the domestic and sexual gifts of their girlfriend—while still enjoying the social and psychological freedom to lead a more independent life. And though LTU implies some kind of committed arrangement, his feelings of vulnerability are in check because he knows they're legally still unhitched. It's like getting the best of both worlds. Are you starting to see how becoming an LTU couple may make a man hesitant to shake his new status quo by proposing? Where's the incentive to change if he's happy with the way things are?

However, don't think we're saying that living together is a totally bad idea. It *can* work, but only if you define what you're hoping to get out of sharing your space. And if marriage and family is your ultimate goal, then you're going to have to keep tabs on the progression of your situation. Otherwise, you may find yourself indefinitely stuck LTU.

Men and Moving In

Simply put, most men place marriage on a higher plane of commitment than simply living together. Accordingly that may make them more willing to jump into a shared-key situation than a 'til-death-do-us-part plan. The thing is, while a woman might think that moving in together is a step in the right direction, many men view LTU as a way of buying time, a test of the possible future, or sadly just a good option until they find the real *one*.

We know what you're thinking: *What do you mean until he finds the* one? *If he wants me to move in, then isn't there a high likelihood that I am that* one? Well, you might be. But you might not be. The problem is, there is no guarantee. And what if you give up your place, move in with your beau, and then find out you're not? You were just the one for right now? Then where will you be?

Keep in mind that it is much harder to extricate yourself from a living-together situation than it is from an exclusive dating scenario. In the latter, you will just need a few Kleenex boxes and some Ben & Jerry's Chunky Monkey coupled with a good cry before you start picking up the pieces. In the former, you'll not only have the need for tissues, ice cream, and tears, but you'll also have to deal with trying to split your stuff and likely find a new place to live. That is a nightmare in the midst of heartbreak.

We're not trying to scare you here. We just want you to think. Like with most of this commitment stuff, women tend to view the progression as a little more linear than men. A woman may be thinking: *We're moving in together—we're on our way!* Whereas he might be reasoning: *We're moving in together—it's going to be great to have regular sex and someone to take care of me for a while.* Get the difference?

By accepting a living-together arrangement, a woman is agreeing to make herself vulnerable, changing her life in the hopes of working toward a future. And while she might be nervous, ultimately she makes peace with the idea because she's been socialized to accept vulnerability as part of the equation for change. A man, on the other hand, sees cohabitation as a way to protect his vulnerability, for now. She's happy because she thinks it means things are going somewhere; he's happy because she's pacified but he hasn't yet had to fully commit. We're not happy because we can see a major domestic disconnect on the horizon—*especially* if there isn't first some kind of discussion about the reasons for living together and a more formal plan for the future. At the very least there better be an honest dialogue about why moving in at this point in the relationship feels right for both parties.

There is another really interesting part of this cohabitation conundrum. When it comes to finding that perfect match—the one person made solely for you—people assume it's typically women seeking out that heavenly coupling. However, more and more studies are showing that men claim to be seeking a "soul mate" just as frequently as women. A man envisions his soul mate as a woman with whom he is completely compatible, someone who he can be himself around with no pretense, someone with whom he can connect on all levels. A man expects his soul mate to willingly take him as he is. He is resistant to change and resistant to someone try-ing to change him. A man will frequently express a desire to find a woman who fits neatly into his life as it already stands. He's not expecting to connect with someone who complains about the way he does the dishes, or how his laundry piles up, or how he never puts the toilet seat back down.

A significant number of male respondents to the National Marriage Project said that part of why they were resisting a marital commitment was that they were not sure if their female cohabitant was their soul mate. They don't want to settle for second best in their choice of a marriage partner. But in the world of double standards, they don't have the same requirements for a choice of a live-in girlfriend. Indeed, in some cases, they see her as a second best partner while they continue to look for a soul mate.

Danger, danger, danger!

Yes, this is exactly the alarm that should be going off in your head about now. What that data alludes to is the idea that a man is actually capable of LTU while still thinking about finding his true love. How can a woman who has put herself in such a situation deal with this uncertainty? Well, for starters, any woman considering moving in with her man must consider the question: Is the push for cohabitation con-venience or commitment?

Cohabitation Is Not Necessarily Commitment

How did we get to this state of cohabitation confusion? Well, for one thing, shacking up has become socially acceptable—according to data from the U.S. Bureau of the Census, there are nearly 5 million nonmarried couples living together in the United Stated today. In fact, LTU has become such a popular form of romantic partnership that slightly more than 44 percent of the twenty- to twenty-nine-year-old single men polled in the National Marriage Project said that they would only marry someone if she agreed to live together first.

Wow, that definitely presents you with a bit of a predicament. In fact, it puts you in a "damned if you do, damned if you don't" position. Why? Well, it says that if you don't live with a man, he might not be interested in marrying you, but if you do live with him, he still might not be interested in marrying you. Even worse, he might end up living with you only to later find someone else to marry. Are you starting to see the pattern here? Though living together may actually serve as a terrific precursor to marriage, it is not necessarily an everlasting commitment. The trick when considering LTU is to make sure you don't set up house prematurely and that you don't jump in without recognizing the risks as well as the possible rewards.

So if a man isn't ready to commit to a woman, what are the reasons he might be willing to commit at least to living with her? Interesting question, and the answers are varied. Sometimes it's *convenience*, sometimes it's *choice*, and sometimes it's *confirmation*. And occasionally it ends up being what the woman was hoping for—a crucial step toward *commitment*.

Convenient Cohabitation

Not surprisingly, men and women often find themselves drifting into LTU in the same way they started dating. It just sort of happens. The problem with this is that while it may seem convenient and easy, it may also be setting the relationship up for miscommunication down the road. The reason? There was never really a discussion about what living together means to either party. Additionally, the reasons for moving in may have less to do with being madly in love or looking toward a promising future, and more to do with "Well, we could save money" or "Her lease is up and it seems like a good idea." The thing that's missing in those statements is any awareness of *why* this is happening in relation to your relationship.

For most women, living together usually signifies something more than combining dishes and linens. But for men, the reasons may be a little more pragmatic. Sorry, we know that dashes the romantic notion that playing house leads to building a life together, but you must be aware of some of the reasons a man will agree or suggest LTU—and very few of them may actually be to help move the relationship forward.

Cashing in on Cohabitation

One big reason men are keen on the idea of LTU is that it is economically viable. This goes hand-in-hand with the fact that one of the biggest turnoffs a man often cites is gold-digging, or a woman only being with him for his money. So, a woman who is willing to step up and take care of her share of the rent may in some way calm his fear that she's just after his wallet, or will lapse from being an independent woman into someone who's looking to be taken care of once married.

The sharing of expenses not only allows the man to feel safer, it also allows him to save money. This combination makes for a win-win situation in his book. With LTU, the guy is able to determine if his girlfriend is willing to contribute her share while simultaneously allowing him to put money away for a rainy day . . . that may or may not be an umbrella for her.

Unfortunately, she probably assumes that rainy day umbrella *will* include her, and if they consolidate their expenses they'll have a better shot at saving for their combined future. Yet another reason for assessing your joint goals *before* accessing joint locks.

An LTU Rationale

A man who isn't sure if he's ready to commit wholly to one woman might also agree to LTU because it allows for a less restricted sex life with his girlfriend. Men believe that they don't have to worry about using condoms if they are in a monogamous LTU relationship. Since they know where their girlfriends are at all times, there's no need to be concerned with STDs. However, there is still the pregnancy issue, but of course, he probably assumes his partner is willing to use a form of birth control, like the pill.

Moreover, a man can avoid the time-consuming effort of figuring out when and where to meet up with his partner for sex since she's living at home with him. Sounds very efficient doesn't it? Instead of upping a man's vulnerability quotient, LTU allows him to have a woman when he wants her, but without feeling like he may never have sex with another woman again—since no vows have been exchanged.

Sadly this way of thinking is not very romantic. A woman would likely be horrified if she thought the reason a guy wanted her to move in was so he could permanently ditch the Magnums, while still keeping open the possibility of using them someday with someone else. However, before you panic and decide that all men are scum, please keep in mind that he may have no intention of pulling out those condoms ever again. It's just the idea that he *could* that makes it easier for him to say "yes" to the idea of living together, even if he's unsure about making it a permanent arrangement. Remember, it's all about understanding the male psyche so he doesn't mess with yours!

The Housekeeping Split

One final addition to the convenience category is that a guy is going to dig having his girlfriend move in with him if she is domestic in any way. Why? Well, what's not to love about someone helping with the chores and everyday household affairs? He doesn't have to hire a housecleaner because he has someone to help him. (Realize we didn't say do *everything* for him—domestic duties should be split fifty-fifty, which is still a huge timesaving advantage for him.) Or if he goes out of town for business, he automatically has someone there to help keep the place running, the pets fed, the plants watered, the mail collected, all the little things. It's like having a quasi-wife, without all the responsibilities that come with the title of husband. And yes, that's a *very* comfortable place for him.

But is it good for you? If you're doing these things under the assumption that it's going somewhere and it's not, well, we're guessing that anger and resentment will start to build up. We'll say it again: If you're moving in, it'll pay off to find out where his head is in the process. We'll help you figure out ways to do that in a bit.

Cohabitation by Choice

You probably think this section is about a woman trying to force a guy to commit by asking to LTU. But, actually, it's not. Women usually are not going to be the ones saying, "I think we should live together instead of getting married." Though she can certainly raise the issue, in many cases, the man gets the idea first. Why? Well, as we've already discussed, it's potentially advantageous for him. It's a way of having you around all the time without having to fully commit (i.e., he's committing to not wanting to lose you—not necessarily committing to you) and finally, society is more accepting of this as a romantic arrangement.

Indeed, as more and more companies begin to loosen the connection between benefits and marriage—meaning domestic partners LTU are treated as if they are actually hitched—it's likely that there may be even higher rates of cohabitation and even lower rates of marriage. This has already happened in Europe, especially in the Northern and Western regions where cohabitation has eclipsed marriage as the first marker for partnership, according to a study done by Kathleen Kiernan for the London School of Economics. In fact, 70 percent of Britains now cohabit prior to marriage. The difference, though, is that many European countries have stronger social safety nets in the form of long, subsidized maternity leave policies; good part-time jobs for mothers; and tight-knit extended families that will help care for children born to single parents.

Changing attitudes about LTU, however, have made it easier for men to see this as a viable option. In fact, men are sometimes encouraged to delay commitment, which is a huge change from years past. Years ago a man in his early twenties would have been given a hard time about having not yet chosen a wife. Today? A man in his twenties might be told not to rush into anything by his peers and mentors. No longer is the single man viewed as not fully matured.

. . . .

Words from the Wise?

Kevin, a twenty-six-year-old go-getter, is rapidly ascending his workplace totem pole and also happens to have found love with a wonderful woman named Katherine. In a display of non-vulnera-phobic male behavior, Kevin mentioned to his boss/mentor, Mark, that he was about ready to take the plunge. It was only *after* they had a conversation, however, that he began thinking that living together might be the more prudent step. Here's Kevin's take on their conversation:

> *I told Mark about my desire to marry Katherine and to my surprise, despite him being in a happy marriage, he asked a whole lot of questions. "What about your plans to upgrade your marketable skills? How well do you really know Katherine? How prepared are you to assume the responsibilities of a husband? Why are you marrying at this time rather than waiting a year or so?" My answer to all of these was the same, "But we are so deeply in love." And Mark's response was that marriage requires much more. He felt that I was setting myself up for a situation that required a dress rehearsal and suggested I try living together as a means to get to know each other even better—as a way to simulate the marriage situation without the full commitment. His counter to me when I said I was concerned how Katherine would take his suggestion was to tell her that LTU demonstrates a great respect and awareness of the seriousness of the marriage commitment.*

....

Is that it? Men think living together really tells a woman he has more respect for marriage? What's more likely in this day and age is that a male has an abject fear of divorce. Many men see living together as a way of avoiding an unhappy marriage. In fact, according to the National Marriage Project, 62 percent of young adults believe that living with someone before marriage is a good way to avoid eventual divorce. So LTU is not only more accepted now—it's encouraged. This is definitely a shift in our nation's social norm.

What's more, men are petrified of the economic ramifications of divorce. Due to the legal and less-permanent ramifications of a living together situation, most men feel that their assets are better protected if they cohabitate rather than marry. Men fear they have more to lose financially from marriage, and this presses them to believe that commitment may not be a prudent move. It goes back to the idea that men are looking at commitment as what they will have to give up and what they might lose instead of focusing on the good things they will gain from a permanent union with a partner.

Therefore, many men feel more comfortable previewing the idea of marriage with a trial run dress rehearsal—which explains why many couples are now viewing living together as just that.

Confirmation Cohabitation

Two people, one roof, no commitment. Will their love survive? You laugh, but cohabitation has become the new experimental engagement.

In fact, men and women are now seeing moving in together as a confirmation that they are seriously considering commitment. It's sort of like those twelve-year-old girls who aren't quite ready for Victoria's Secret lingerie so they give them training bras in a section called "preteen." Think baby steps toward something grown-up. The same premise applies to those in the maybe-we-should-live-together-first department. You're moving toward being in a full-fledged committed adult relationship but trying it on for size first.

At least that's how a huge number of people are coming to view LTU. It's a seemingly safe intermediary step between "we're an item" and "we're together forever." But can living together really serve as a sort of teething phase for the real thing?

Actually, it can be a step in the permanent direction as more and more people are coming to regard LTU as a laboratory in which new ways of relating can be put into practice. The very nature of the closeness allows a couple to offer each other feedback so that they may recognize and modify relationship-defeating behaviors. Living together can provide the permissive, nonpressured kind of atmosphere needed to help sort out mixed feelings, to come to terms with unrealistic expectations, and to know and become known by another person on more intimate terms. If approached with awareness, it can broaden a person's education no matter if the relationship is continued, dissolved, or is an interlude before marriage.

The caveat in the above statement, however, is that there has to be mutual awareness that this arrangement is being undertaken as a possible confirmation of long-term compatibility (or conversely, a refutation for the idea that total togetherness should be the couple's eventual path). If living together is a "test," then both parties must be privy to the "petri dish" nature of their bathroom-sharing behavior.

Simply moving in with another person does not automatically ensure any of the benefits previously mentioned. Whether it be in marriage or a less formal commitment, the experience of living with another person requires effort and realistic expectations. While practically every LTU situation (and every marriage) contains elements of convenience, some of these factors—including shacking up just to share expenses or delay commitment—may be warning signs. This is especially true when the motive is not really practice for an everlasting commitment, or when one partner (typically her) is firm about an eventual marriage but the other is quite happy leaving the arrangement as is. Sometimes, however, both halves of a twosome may be on the same page about moving in together and this is when it can serve as a very healthy step in a relationship's progression.

. . . .

Taking the Risk

Jennifer and Allan decided to live together after having known each other for over a year. Their report, after six months of cohabitation, illustrates the creative use of this option as a bridge to a new commitment. Jennifer reveals:

We wanted something more than our dating relationship was affording us. Both of us looked forward to being able to share our lives with each other. Despite high hopes, though, we had many fears and uncertainties: Would the realities of stronger obligations to each other crush the friendship we had achieved? Would the day in, day out contact leave us bored? Would we expose each other to annoying habits, yet unseen? There was really no way to tell until we took the risk. The only thing we were sure of was that we enjoyed each other's company immensely and that we were not yet prepared to marry. Neither of us trusted ourselves enough to say with finality that we could tolerate the other's idiosyncrasies and work out differences between us satisfactorily. We just did not have enough of that kind of experience with each other. Living together, we hoped, would give us that experience. Several basic guidelines were established: We agreed the relationship would be monogamous; it would have no time limit nor would it necessarily result in marriage; and, since both of us worked, we agreed to share household tasks equally.

After about three months I had fallen into a familiar trap. I was playing the compliant, ever-giving female—taking Allen's lead even when it conflicted with what I really wanted. Whether it was going out with his friends, listening to his choice of music, or eating what he wanted for dinner, it seemed I was always deferring to his preference. I would always go along with things like a nice little girl. Isn't that how to keep a man's love? At least that's what I grew up believing—foolishly. I didn't want to replicate my mother's life. Remembering the pain in my parent's marriage helped me work up the courage to discuss these things with Allen. Because of this issue, I had a great deal of resentment and there was a mounting tension between us.

To my surprise, Allen was not rejecting but rather encouraged me to speak up. Even if our relationship had not lasted, that part of my experience with Allen, where I was able for the first time to express myself openly, strengthened me enormously and was worth the risk.

Living together enabled Jennifer and Allen to move in the direction of increased involvement that eventually led to marriage.

....

For others, living together may not result in marriage but rather in a decision to separate. And, for women whose goal is definitely marriage, the big risk is: Will he become so comfortable with the benefits of living together that he won't have motivation to take the next step? There's no way to eliminate that risk. The best a marriage-minded woman can do is to make sure she moves into a LTU arrangement for the right reasons—or if the risk still keeps her up nights, not move in at all, holding out for that final commitment step, marriage.

Moving in or Moving on

The good news is that there is at least the possibility that the ultimate commitment may spring from cohabitation. But in order to make sure that you aren't one of those women who finds herself moving in but not moving forward, you should learn some of the elements that might lead to successfully LTU. With that in mind, consider the following questions when contemplating cohabitation.

Has he ever lived with another woman before? How many times? Cohabitation experiences play a growing role in the marriage attitudes of today's unmarried men. Close to a third of the men in the National Marriage Project study say that they have lived with a woman in the past or are currently cohabiting with a girlfriend. What is more important here, however, is that the men who have had only one live-in relationship or are currently in their first live-in relationship are more likely to agree with the statement "Your most important personal goal is getting married," compared to men with no living-together experience or those with more than one cohabitation experience. This view probably reflects the new socially accepted role that cohabitation now plays as a stepping stone into marriage. Half of marriages today are preceded by cohabiting unions. But if he's a serial cohabiter, tread carefully.

Are your reasons for moving in together based on something other than a desire to be closer? Financial savings, convenience, regular sex, avoiding a fuller commitment for the time being—each of these independently may not be a big enough reason to worry about agreeing to LTU. But a smart woman should be aware that any or all of these as a *primary* basis for LTU could indicate that moving in may not actually be moving things toward the alter. If marriage is your goal, make sure that you discuss why you're shacking up before you set up house. You need to know his reasons for wanting to make this move.

Have you discussed his feelings on marriage? The National Marriage Project found that young men are reluctant to marry because just living with a woman is easier. Several men expressed the opinion that there was little difference between the commitment to live together and the commitment to marriage. According to them, marriage is "just a piece of paper," a "legal thing" that you do for family and friends. One observed that cohabitation was just like being married, so why go through the hassle of an expensive ceremony and legal contract? The good news is that this was a minority of men. However, that still means there are men out there operating under this mindset. Make sure you know where your guy stands *before* you get in too deep.

Do you find yourself falling into typical female stereotypes when you stay over for more than a day? If you recognize that you're doing all the cleaning up around his place or always cooking for him, his idea of how great it would be for you to move in may be less linked to your fabulous mutual connection and more tied to the idea of having a quasi-wife in place for a while—whether or not you end up his forever-wife. Pay attention to your own behavior when you're around him and see if you're making things so easy for him in a LTU arrangement that he won't feel a need to commit.

What are your expectations concerning cohabitation? You need to make sure you have articulated these to your partner.

Do you think living together is a step toward marriage? Or are you okay with it being just a living arrangement with no promise of anything? Maybe this is supposed to act as a test for you as much as it is for him. Be honest with these thoughts and then share them with your partner before you move in together. It's important to know your own expectations going in, or no matter what happens, the experience will be a letdown for you.

These discussions and even eventual cohabitation can be a great thing for your relationship if—and we reiterate *if*—you follow these guidelines and make sure you know what you're getting into. Don't just drift into LTU if marriage is your goal. Be smart or you might find yourself locked out of your own matrimonial dream. And that's just not nice, which brings us to our next chapter. One big part of commitment is thoughtfulness toward your partner and vice versa. A truly committed man is going to think about you and your well-being as if it were his own. Read on to see why sometimes nice guys finish first (or at least get married first).

THE COMMITMENT-READY MAN ... Will suggest moving in together as a way of advancing the relationship, not for reasons such as economic viability or convenience. He will recognize this as a step toward something permanent and will be willing to discuss this openly before a woman agrees to try the arrangement without a ring.

COMMITMENT
Is Thoughtfulness

Does he remember your birthday? Anniversary? How you met? Does he follow up when you tell him you have something important pending like your mother's biopsy or your big job review? Does he call when he says he will? Does he ask you about your day?

If you answer "no" to more than one of the previous questions, you might be in a lopsided relationship. And as you might guess, commitment is pretty tough when it's a party of one.

Thoughtfulness is a pivotal element in any potential long-term pairing. There is no way around this. If two people are committed to each other, they should care what happens to the other person. They should want that person to feel special, protected, loved. Tuning into the little things as well as the major events is what makes this happen. It's paying attention to the fabric of the other person's life, and in so doing becoming an interwoven part of that material.

In fact, thoughtfulness is one of the major hallmarks of someone who cares about you. Basically, the actively caring person can be thought of as a supply source of satisfaction. And not surprisingly, most of us are drawn to these types of suppliers—people who act positively toward us. It is in this atmosphere that women feel valued.

The problem is that during the hot period in the relationship a man is more likely to be thoughtful. Keep in mind, however, that his caring may be lust driven. And if it gets him into bed with you, he'll keep doing it because it works. But how do you know if he's being attentive to get a between-the-sheets session or if his thoughtful behavior indicates true commitment potential? It's a hard thing to figure out. So, we decided to explore the ways thoughtfulness manifests in relationships and what it means for your commitment prospects.

Commitment Is Action, Not Words

Here's a little hint: Believe what a man does, not what he says. Players know how to manipulate you verbally. Partners know how to cherish you tangibly. And in that difference lays the key to commitment potential.

Why is this? Well, on the whole men are much more behavior oriented than women. Think about it: men are taught to be doers. They fix things and they take action when they want something. So in their minds, when it comes to expressing affection, a man who is really into a girl will probably show it way before he says it. He may still dish out the compliments, but if he doesn't, women shouldn't necessarily think that he's indifferent—it just may not be his style. And seriously, how many men do you know that are terrific communicators? There are some, of course, but most of the time it is women who are the more verbal sex.

A man who is invested in his girlfriend will not only tell her she's beautiful, he'll *make* her feel beautiful. How so? By giving her the love and support that will enable her to shine. Commitment is not about empty compliments. Women thrive when they know they are adored, respected, and cherished. And ultimately that comes from feeling supported.

Ironically, however, many women don't realize this fact. A lot of single women pay more attention to what men say than what they do. Women need to hear affirmations that they are lovely and loved. But in so doing, many women are putting the emphasis on the wrong barometer when it comes to gauging their future happiness.

Another important thing to keep in mind is that often-times in relationships, men and women have different goals. And while men may typically be action oriented, it pays to try to discern if the goal of his actions is more about making the woman feel secure and loved than getting some action (yes, we're referring back to the "commitment is more than just sex" stuff here). Arguably, it can be hard to tell. There are some real charmers out there. And the worst part, sometimes they're so good they may even have themselves fooled.

That said, a commitment-seeking woman would do well to look at what a man she's dating does rather than what he says as an indicator of his vulnera-phobia, or lack thereof. It's in a man's behavior and actions that a woman will get a better sense of where her man's heart is. And, the best indica-tor is a bit later in the relationship (i.e., past the sex in the hallway stage).

Also, pay attention to the little things he does, not just the grandstanding. He might buy you a bike for your birth-day or a Tiffany necklace for Valentine's Day, and those are wonderful gifts, but a woman would do well to notice if he remembers to ask how her important meeting went or takes her dry-cleaning to be done when he takes his own. These smaller actions show that he's looking out for her day-to-day well-being as well, and that's the sign of someone on the commitment path. Basically, it boils down to: He cares, so he does.

JUST SAY IT!

Without getting all Mars and Venus on you, we wanted to include the following true story because it illustrates how this comes into play in the real world. A woman goes into the hospital with what might be a serious illness. While hospitalized, her husband goes to work, as well as takes care of the kids and household, and visits with his wife late into every night.

Fortunately for the whole family, it turns out the woman is fine, so she's discharged from the hospital. On the way home she turns to her completely exhausted husband and tells him, "I could have had a life-threatening illness and you didn't tell me you loved me even once!" The husband is very taken back. "I was at the hospital every single night, I took care of the kids and the house, I went to work to pay the bills—doesn't all that show love?"

Her response? "But, I had to *hear* it. I need to hear the words, 'I love you.'"

It's a fundamental difference in the sexes. A man thinks if he's providing and caring, the woman will automatically know that he loves her. Women, on the other hand, really want verbal reassurance as well (again, generally women are the more communicative sex). And there is nothing wrong with that. However, a smart woman should recognize that words and promises can be empty and that within the context of behaviors, she may ultimately be getting all the love signals she needs.

Women still on the dating scene should definitely be alert to the fact that they may be unduly swayed by words as well.

Why do you think someone coined the phrase "He's such a smooth talker"? The man who knows all the right things to say is oftentimes also the man who knows how to reel in women by the dozen. That's not to say that every member of the male species blessed with the gift of the gab is a player; we're just putting you on high alert because as a whole, women tend to be more susceptible to linguistic persuasion.

But just when you think you have it all figured out, there will be something that seemingly breaks that rule as well.

....

All Is Not as It Seems — Sometimes

Consider Carrie and Jeffrey. Carrie is a thirty-three-year-old event planner and Jeffrey runs a small agency. They've been dating on-and-off for over two years. When it comes to action, Jeffrey is giving off all the right signals. He clearly adores Carrie and his behavior confirms his affection, but in his case his words don't support it.

> *Jeffrey is the type of guy who tells me he doesn't know how he feels about me, as he's simultaneously wrapping me in his arms, covering me with kisses, and then picking me up and bringing me to the bed. He always calls back, e-mails fifty times a day, and has never once blown me off. But he'll say things like, "Sometimes I want to be with you, sometimes I don't."*
>
> *Also, he told me that he used to tell his ex-girlfriend he loved her but he has never said this to me except once in his sleep. Is it a coincidence that his ex was a twenty-one-year-old Russian girl and they barely spoke the same language? I think not! Easier to say to someone*

you can't really have a deep connection with except on a superficial level.

We wanted to include Carrie's example because it shows that nothing in life or commitment is linear and that vulneraphobia can manifest in different ways. Jeffrey's actions do suggest that he loves Carrie. And chances are he really is smitten. However, his fear of commitment is causing him to use words to help him keep a safe distance (or at least make him feel as if he is). So actions are still speaking louder than words here, but his words are not supporting his actions and thus causing Carrie major confusion. In this case, Carrie could choose to hang in there and see if he ever manages to get over his fear of commitment, because even though his insecurities are showing up loud and clear in his inability to commit, there is at least the suggestion of real love by his behaviors. However, if he can't bust through his walls soon, Carrie may have to move on. You can't force a man to commit—even if he does love you.

. . . .

Also keep in mind that in the beginning of any relationship, chances are the tangible displays of affection will be numerous—flowers, romantic dinners, unexpected gifts. The flourish factor is usually in full effect. And while these things are undoubtedly awesome (what woman doesn't love being spoiled a bit?), remember that they are also part of the action-oriented goal-seeking behavior of your date—he knows that in order to woo you, he must give a little. At this point in the process, his actions are speaking toward a goal, not so much toward future commitment. He's trying to win you, and men like to win. It's a challenge; it's part of the game. So, you can enjoy his actions for now, but don't put too much stock in any of them just yet.

The real test happens when you've been dating for a while, because that is when his mannerisms will either become more genuine or taper off a bit. Unfortunately, a woman may be so in love at this point that she doesn't recognize that his actions are no longer supporting his words. But there are definitely some clues. When deciding for yourself if the man you are seeing has true commitment potential, consider some of the following signs that he wants you only on his terms:

He begins to find fault with you, not occasionally, but frequently. This usually starts small, but if you notice that he is suddenly getting annoyed at your little quirks (the ones he used to cherish) it might be a sign that while he's into you, it's not unconditional. He loves having you around; he wants to be with you—as long as you're perfect. Anything that shows up as a little blip in your supposedly ideal relationship will start to cause him concern, and he will begin to point out these things in order to pave the way for his exit should he decide that you are getting too close or someone better comes along.

He starts flirting with other women and even going on dates, maybe in hopes that you will catch him and break it off. This includes online perusing too. Though he may not have actually met anyone yet, if he's looking or maybe even posting a personal ad, it can be considered bad boyfriend behavior. Surprisingly, if you do catch him he may cry and beg for forgiveness. But that's not love. He simply can't commit to *not* having you. And that anti-action says it all.

He spends less and less time with you. It used to be that he wanted your every Friday, Saturday, and Sunday night. And you willingly set aside that part of your week as couple time. But then all of a sudden he starts having to go out with his former boss who is visiting from out of state or his best pal from the gym—and you're not invited. Though allowing him "guy time" is important, a sudden shift in your inclusion may definitely indicate that he may still want you, but only when it fits into his schedule. And don't you want a partner who wants you all the time, not just when it's convenient?

He ignores your needs and wants—even more than he's done in the past. In the beginning, chances are your wish was his command . . . as long as it led the relationship toward the bedroom. But as you've settled in to a relationship, you notice that your needs are suddenly becoming secondary to his. This is a sign that this relationship is lopsided. In a true partnership with long-lasting potential, both partners still look out for themselves but they also place equal—if not heightened—importance on the wishes of their loved one.

Though he's still giving you gifts, you can sense that they are being doled out for appearance's sake more than out of genuine caring. You can tell when a gift is selected especially for you and when a gift is picked out just because he was like "Oh, I should give her a gift." There is a difference. Does he listen to what you say? Does he know that you like white chocolate over dark, and then chooses your Godiva accordingly? If you start to receive presents that have nothing to do with your true self and preferences, chances are he's not really paying attention to you either. You'll understand the difference—a woman just knows.

When you have little disagreements, he tries to change the subject, makes a quick escape, or deflects the blame. A guy who wants you when he wants you is not going to be very keen to work out any disagreements you have or take responsibility for his own behavior. He's just going to want you to go away until the whole thing blows over and you two can have fun again. In other words, he's not really looking for a real relationship because, like it or not, relationships are work. Any man who gets defensive or unwilling to put in the time for real conflict resolution is likely looking at his girlfriend as a short-term distraction, not a long-term partner.

He expects you to do all the bending and accommodating to make the relationship work. If a man wants you to fit neatly into his life and isn't doing enough bending on his end, it's a big neon sign that he wants you, but only if it's not an inconvenience to him. Are you always going to his place instead of him coming to yours? Are you changing your plans to fit his schedule? Are you meeting up with his friends more than yours? Are you agreeing to activities you may not necessarily enjoy just because it's what he wants to do? Keep in mind that in a true partnership, both parties must learn to give and take. If he's not willing to be flexible for you sometimes, he wants you on his terms, which is self-centered.

While none of these are foolproof indicators that your man lacks the caring qualities needed to commit, if these signs start to show up in increasing numbers, it might be time to take stock of the relationship and to decide if this man is in this relationship for you or for himself. If it's the latter, you might be dealing with one of the ultimate vulnera-phobic types, the narcissist. And these men are *dangerous*, because they're charming, smart, and likely to suck you in quick, but ultimately break your heart.

The Vulnera-Phobic Narcissist

When you hear the word *narcissist* you probably think of someone who can't stop staring at himself, right? Well, this personality type is actually a lot more complicated than that. In fact, that's precisely why the vulnera-phobic narcissist (VN) can cause turmoil in any single woman's life. This type of man is usually charming, witty, smart, good-looking, successful, and on the surface even seems to be incredibly thoughtful. In fact, he's so good at appearing thoughtful he may even manage to fool himself. But the bottom line? The VN is really in a relationship for his own benefit. If he gives, it's because inherently (if not subconsciously) he knows it'll make it easier for him to get what he wants. And frequently women don't realize they're with a faux-giver until they're so much in love, they miss the clues.

So what are the key points of a VN? Well, aside from the usual vulnera-phobic tendencies like an inability to commit or get too close in a relationship for fear of appearing weak or feeling out of control of his emotions, the VN usually has suffered some kind of narcissistic wound early in his life. For example, he may have experienced the death of a parent and as a result didn't get the attention he needed as a child. However, that injury doesn't have to be a headline maker either. The issue is fundamentally that the future VN has some very strong emotional needs that don't get adequately met for whatever reason.

Fast-forward many years into the future, and the VN has probably grown up to be a successful man (you'll find a lot of VNs in the entertainment business or working as litigators—anywhere they can get onstage) and is frequently very charming, personable, and charismatic. There is an aggressiveness made acceptable because of his charm. This aggressiveness comes from a sense of entitlement—this is *big* with VNs—but, again, it is made acceptable and toned down because of his charm.

And the VN tendency will be heightened even further if later in life that person is betrayed, like by a girlfriend or wife who steps out on him in some way. That kind of disloyalty will reopen the VN's childhood wound, morphing it into a gaping hole that may never heal—at least not without a very understanding partner and a wickedly sharp therapist. And the wound will be all that much deeper if it is inflicted by someone with whom they have allowed themselves to be vulnerable, because that would be the ultimate betrayal of their fragile inner world. This man may appear together on the outside, but feeling vulnerable on the inside is a worse fate than death for the VN. So, all his consequent actions will be motivated by an intense drive to keep any feelings of vulnerability and weakness at bay.

The point is, VNs do not take rejection well, and therefore vulnera-phobia runs through narcissists like a typhoon. However, it is usually not immediately obvious because they have adapted to keeping it away so well—while their vulnerability is raging, it is masked by charm, guile, and practice from a lifetime of keeping it at bay.

How do VNs manage to squash their feelings of vulnerability? Well, to begin with, in one way or another these guys need to feel special—that's what drives them to be successful—and they believe, often subconsciously, that success will keep the V-monster away. So, while VNs may be found in any occupation, they are usually high up. And the ones most difficult to see through are the really intelligent ones. Actually, many of them are quite bright, another engaging factor, which when combined with the charm, subtle aggressiveness, charisma, and success these guys frequently possess allows them to draw women in by the dozens.

That leads to the next point: VNs are often players. But they're particularly dangerous because they don't come off as players to the untrained female eye. In fact, they are the best players on the planet because of their ability to emulate sincerity. And they are so good at it because they don't really know they're faking—it feels totally real to them. So they are literally able to charm the pants off a woman with their actions and truly believe that they are invested in the relationship.

In reality their behavior is all in the interest of making them feel special, thus keeping their own feelings of vulnerability suppressed. When it comes to a VN, he may be superficially thoughtful—but down the line it will be *all* about him. Well, not *all*; he'll give you just enough to keep you interested in him—and to keep you giving him what he wants.

While it can be hard to spot a VN immediately, a woman should be aware of this type of man, because a VN is a poor commitment risk. If you are dealing with a true VN, eventually the traits will start to surface (even if they're well hidden in the beginning of the relationship). Keep the following in mind:

A VN will frequently exhibit a subtle sense of entitlement. He likely feels he "deserves" certain things, likes to buy himself expensive presents, and might even call himself "spoiled." This may trickle over into what he thinks he should get from you as his girlfriend, and if he stops getting it, he'll move on.

A VN displays a very good but *faked* sense of empathy. The VN can be very sympathetic, but that is different from empathetic; internally they are never in the other person's shoes—it's *always* ultimately about them.

A VN is a master manipulator. He's so good in fact, it's scary, because he'll start to make you feel like it might be your fault that he's not doing things for you as frequently, or not committing to you. Remember, it's not you. He's just more concerned about himself.

VNs tend not to value relationships unless it's for self-serving purposes. Otherwise, why would they risk getting close to someone? Remember, their goal is to keep vulnerability as far away as possible.

There is one more important thing to keep in mind with VNs, and that's how they perceive sex. A recent study from the University of Florida showed that narcissists not only have a heightened sense of sexuality, but they also view sex very differently than other people. VNs see sexuality more in terms of power and influence, and as something daring, as opposed to people with low narcissistic qualities, who associate sex more with caring and love. As a result, VNs are more likely to go through a string of short-term relationships (and are more predisposed to philandering and dumping their partners) than people who view closeness and commitment as the hallmarks of a good relationship.

When you consider how intimate sex can be, it would make sense that the VN—who has an abject fear of letting himself feel vulnerable—would want to make sex as athletic, rough, or unconnected as possible. Building on that thought, we move on to another important commitment sign: his bedroom behavior.

Thoughtfulness in the Bedroom

Are you more often than not left unsatisfied after sex with your lover? Does he seem unconcerned about that? Is that throwing doubt into your hopes for commitment?

The way a man behaves in the bedroom is absolutely telling of where your relationship may be headed. Though like everything in life, some guys are simply better in bed than others, the bottom line is that the man who is looking for something more than a partner for regular sack sessions is going to behave differently than the man who is only about satisfying his carnal desires. If you're left cold after sex (or hot but not finished) while he's passing out, then thoughtfulness has left the bedroom and you need to think twice about where your relationship is headed.

Here's the thing: Men view sex differently than women. That we've already established. In fact, many men may be able to look at sex like a sport. They push hard, reach a goal, and then hit the locker room for a shower (or the kitchen for a snack). And occasionally it's okay for a woman to accept sex that is all about his pleasure. But we stress the word *occasionally*. Why? Because too many women are willing to put up with it being all about his pleasure *frequently* or *most of the time*. However, there is a little something called *reciprocity* that women sometimes forget, but it must be considered if commitment is your ultimate goal.

You see, the man who is really looking to be with you for the long term is also going to be the man who wants to please you in bed. In other words, if he's all into his own kinks and pleasure and forgets about you (the beautiful woman underneath him) in the process, it's likely that he's not really thinking about your well-being outside of the bedroom. The man who realizes what a prize you are will remember that even in the heat of passion. He'll want to build you up and make you feel adored while also satisfying his manly needs. In other words, he's going to want to "give" in bed because it makes you feel good, not just because it ensures that he'll get what he wants. True thoughtfulness doesn't have a price tag attached.

As we discussed previously in regard to VNs, it's also important for you as a commitment-seeking woman to remember that committed sex includes having sex in a way that nurtures and builds trust and communication between two people. It's an intimate connection that fosters closeness, love, and caring. If you find yourself in a situation where that is never or rarely happening, you may start to feel yourself pulling away outside the bedroom as well. Why? Because your emotional and physical needs are not being met during sex (and like it or not, sex is a big part of any relationship). A man who is truly desirous of a long-term commitment is going to be aware of how his woman is responding in bed, what her needs are, what makes her happy. He's going to try to figure out what gives her pleasure as well as him. Being a thoughtful lover means a man must remember that there is another person involved in the sexual experience as well. A woman is not just a prop to help him scale his peak.

....

Sparks that Turn to Embers

Consider Katie, a thirty-five-year-old woman in a relationship with a dashing, but likely VN, named Matt. In the beginning of their relationship, the sex was amazing. It was reciprocal and connected and Katie fell hard and fast for this man. But once the initial infatuation stage began to wear off, Katie noticed a shift in Matt's sexual behavior that caused her concern. Suddenly their relationship, which had been seemingly perfect, began to show cracks:

When I first met Matt, I couldn't believe how fantastic things were. Not only was he smart and good-looking but when we kissed, it was electric. Not surprisingly we found our way into bed after about four fabulous dates. And our connection there seemed even more perfect. For months we happily sailed down this incredible relationship path that seemed destined for a committed ending. Matt even said that he knew we'd end up together. It seemed like I'd found "The One."

But then at about the six-month mark, our relationship emerged from the honeymoon phase and suddenly I also noticed that Matt started to forget about me during sex. I guess he thought that now that he had me hooked he could relax. But the bigger problem with this new sack development was that my once-thoughtful lover started to treat me like a toy. I was no longer a part of the equation. He tried to push my limits, focusing on his sexual preferences, some of them rough, every time we had sex and my pleasure was definitely put on the backburner. I ended up feeling hurt, emotionally and sometimes even physically. I became confused and it did start to affect our relationship outside of sex because I kept thinking, "How is it possible that this man who says he loves me so much has forgotten about making me feel good?" It made me start to question everything—in and out of bed.

. . . .

Katie was right to question her relationship with Matt. When a man forgets about his partner in bed, it's a red flag. Commitment includes caring about how you feel during sex. No doubt lovemaking is a very important part of your relationship, but it takes two to tango. If he seemingly doesn't give a damn about your pleasure that may indicate more about his commitment prospects than simply being a bad or selfish lover. Any guy who truly cares and suspects that he might be leaving his lover in the lurch, sexually speaking, would try to compensate in some way. In the end Katie left Matt and was heartbroken, but his bedroom behavior showed that he was ultimately not in the relationship for her anymore.

When considering how your own sex life stacks up and how it might intersect with your commitment desires, it might be helpful to think about some of the following suggestions:

Don't delude yourself into thinking he's commitment material just because he's terrific in the sack. For many women, giving themselves to a man sexually jumpstarts thoughts about commitment, especially if he's really good in bed. Of course, there are those times when both men and women consider a sexual experience as being nothing more than a tryst. Those kinds of situations aside, women who desire a serious relationship with a man tend to assume that if they are having an ongoing sexual relationship it carries the consideration of commitment.

The rub is that most men who enjoy their sexual encounters with a woman do not necessarily feel that way. Generally speaking, the majority of men do not equate sex with commitment. They equate sex with sex. There's still a serious disconnect between the sexes and, agree with it or not, that's the way that it is in most cases.

Don't assume he should know—and care—about how you feel about the lovemaking. It's a mistake to take for granted that he knows how you feel about your sex life if you haven't told him. For couples who've been together for some time, talking about sex is often given less time than talking about the functions on your cell phone.

As we've discussed, if there's no conversation between you and your guy, it is likely that you'll have one with yourself instead, which will likely generate bad feelings and resentment. If you are desirous of commitment, talk about the sexual issues in an effort to give you a better sense of what's going on, rather than drawing your own, perhaps mistaken, conclusions. How your guy responds will be telling.

Don't assume that sudden awkwardness in your sex life means that things are fizzling out. The irony is that lovemaking is often more uninhibited at the beginning of a relationship when you don't know each other well. After a while, if the relationship becomes more important, there's more on the line; shyness and awkwardness often set in. If this is what's happened, rather than conclude he's not into you anymore, push yourself to have a talk about it. Don't have the courage? Get a good sexy book, highlight the parts you find hot, and leave it for your guy. After seeing what you've highlighted, it should prompt change. If not, why not?

Don't expect a man to take care of you sexually and otherwise. Expectation may lead you to feel entitled to other perks—and entitlement is almost always a mistake. Don't expect a man to take care of things if you're not able to take care of your own things. Go out and get your own career, take care of yourself, pay your own bills, buy a vibrator, and stop looking for some guy who's going to do everything for you. That action alone will probably notch down his fear of commitment.

Do remember that sex isn't always intimate and intimacy doesn't necessarily involve sex. If your guy says he's interested in you for the long term, and both of you want that commitment to have juice, ask yourself if he's sharing himself with you. A critical factor to long-term commitment is whether he shares his heart. Some men, even when they live with someone, are often really living alone. They don't share their thoughts and intimate feelings for fear that their partner might use what they expose against them. They keep themselves busy at work or become so involved in other activities—sports, the gym, buddies—that there isn't much time or energy left for intimacy. If the intimacy isn't there, it won't be long before the commitment isn't there either.

So as you can see, what on the surface may appear to be a simple issue can lead to all kinds of complexity. Bedroom behavior is a gateway to the inner struggle men are having with commitment. A substantial number of men today are coping with the questions of how to be selfish without being considered wholly self-interested and how to be selfless without running the risk of losing their sense of self. But, in the end, the ones who are looking for more than sexual gratification in a relationship will be the ones who also want to make sure their partner feels cherished, adored, and supported during sex.

Thoughtfulness in bed—past the infatuation stage when he might be trying to please you in order to ensure he gets what he wants—is definitely an indication that a man is looking for something more than just a sexual relationship. If he's committed to you outside of the bedroom, it'll show up as commitment to your satisfaction between the sheets as well. And that's not something that should ever be make-believe.

Pseudo-Benevolence

This chapter would not be complete without some space devoted to what we call the emotional equivalent of faking an orgasm: pseudo-benevolence. Sometimes people in relationships get confused and what they think is thoughtful behavior toward their partner is actually altruism on their own behalf. Like the guy who buys something for your birthday that he would like—he doesn't get it; it's your birthday and not his.

....

The Golden Rule Disconnect

Consider Susan and Gary, he's a thirty-four-year-old attorney and she's a thirty-two-year-old librarian, and they have been engaged for nearly a year. Gary expresses his caring in practical, sensible ways: instead of bringing flowers, which soon wilt, he brings home new kitchen gadgets; rather than phoning from the office, he works straight through and often quite late, hoping to earn a promotion. To Gary these are caring expressions.

But to Susan, someone who doesn't enjoy time in the kitchen and is opposed to making more money at the expense of time together, his efforts go unappreciated. She's more sentimental, less practical. It feels to her that his caring is really about him, not her.

This may be one situation where the golden rule—"Do unto others as you would have others do unto you"—is not the right approach. Gary supposedly believes that he is behaving in a loving, benevolent manner toward Susan. In reality, he is behaving in an insensitive, even selfish, manner, "If it pleases me, it should please you").

. . . .

This kind of thoughtfulness disconnect can lead to definite long-term issues for couples. When it comes to looking for a real committed relationship, it's not just about identifying thoughtfulness in your partner; it's about making sure that your partner is being thoughtful in ways that actually promote a growth-supporting, loving atmosphere for you. True thoughtfulness is when the person you are with keys into your needs and desires as well as his own (and recognizes that they may be different).

Bottom line: When it comes to thoughtfulness, we're not talking about finding a guy who is destined for sainthood. He doesn't exist. Everyone (even you) screws up. Everyone has a self-centered element to his or her personality. But a guy who has a pattern of caring behavior that continues beyond infatuation has potential, especially if that thoughtfulness extends beyond you to include your family and friends (which we'll discuss further in Chapter 7).

THE COMMITMENT-READY MAN ... Is willing to put your needs on an equal plane with his own because he has realized that his happiness is intrinsically linked with yours. His thoughtfulness is not just motivated by a desire to satisfy his own needs, but also by a true desire to make you feel cherished and loved. And it's not in the grandstanding, it's in the everyday ways he makes you feel supported.

7

COMMITMENT
Is Integration of Lives

*A*s two people start to become one, there is a lot of blending that goes into the mix. You have to remember, when it comes to relationships, it's not just about the two of you. Lovely as it might be to live in a happy little cocoon for the rest of your lives, the true mark of a good relationship is when both parties are open to sharing their own lives with their significant other. In a sense, that means becoming conjoined—partners with a combined circle of friends, family, acquaintances, and interests.

Unless you've managed to meet a total introvert, chances are that just like you, the man in your life has his own circle—friends that he hung out with before he met you, his family, work colleagues, and soon, as you become more and more a part of his life, it should be natural that you start to meet this circle. In fact, if he's at all excited about you, he's going to want to show you off to them. After a while, they may also start to become part of your circle.

Bottom line: No man is an island. Therefore, no couple that hopes to make it for the long term should act like they're stranded on one. Before you came together, you had lives.

And in looking at how you mesh them, you'll find clues as to where your relationship may be headed.

Commitment Means Meeting the Friends

So here's the thing: If a man is into you, you're going to be spending a lot of time with him, which means you'll be meeting some of his friends. If you don't, there is definitely something wrong with your relationship. A guy who is into you is not going to want to hide you. Why? Well, your very presence ups how cool he's perceived by his friends.

So if after a month of dating you haven't met at least one of his pals, you might want to subtly ask when you get to meet Matt, John, Jim, Eric, Scott, or any other guy he's mentioned more than once. Your guy's reaction will be telling. If he doesn't jump at the chance or at least say how much he's looking forward to having you meet his buds at some point, you may want to seriously question your status (we're guessing he views you as a hookup not a girlfriend).

Another thing to consider: A recent study published by the American Psychological Association showed that men who were closer to their friends as teens were more expressive and emotionally attached to their romantic partners in early adulthood. In other words, instead of being threatened that your guy has a strong circle of friends, you should be encouraged because it shows he's loyal and is capable of forming close bonds with others. His close relations can translate into a closer relationship with you as well.

Of course, this comes with a caveat. If your guy's relationship with his pals is taking precedence over your relationship, then there could be some rough times ahead.

....

Spending the Holidays Apart?

Consider Julie, thirty-six years old and a stock trader, who is freaking out about her boyfriend's sudden change of holiday plans, which don't seem to include her:

My boyfriend of a year, Mark, just told me he is going on a trip across the country with a bunch of his guy friends, which is fine except that he wants to go over New Year's! I would understand if he wanted to go away on a normal weekend, but this is a special occasion. Am I wrong for being upset? I believe that couples, especially serious couples, should be together for the holidays. Plus, my mother says that if I let him do this, he will run over me for the rest of our lives. I keep telling myself that if he goes through with this, I will break up with him when he comes back.

....

For many people, the holiday season is a time to evaluate their lives, jobs, and relationships, and to make important decisions about whether to go forward or let go. Therefore, if a man chooses to be with a bunch of his guy friends instead of his girlfriend on a major holiday like New Year's, it's a pretty clear statement of where his priorities lie. While it may seem that he simply prefers being with them on this outing, the truth may be deeper: He may actually have a hankering to be single again.

People often fluctuate between moving ahead with a relationship and going back to their freedom. Therefore, it's important and empowering for a woman when faced with a situation like this to not just capitulate but rather use it as an opportunity to examine her significant other's behavior in general. She should seriously ask herself if she sees the characteristics in this man that she wishes to have in a partner for life.

In the case of Julie and Mark, if Julie lets Mark know that it upsets her that he wants to spend New Year's without her but he chooses to go anyway despite how she feels, then she is dealing with a larger problem: He doesn't take her feelings and needs into account. The foundation of a successful relationship is mutual respect and consideration for each other's feelings. To just take off without her indicates a lack of compassion. Not to mention a lack of maturity as well. It might also be a backdoor tactic to make her angry enough to break up with him because he doesn't have the decency to do it himself.

Bottom line: You don't want a relationship with someone you have to manage or threaten by allowing him to do this or that. You want a relationship where there is mutual goodwill and understanding, which includes putting your needs higher than that of his posse.

Responsive vs. Reactive

If all of your man's friends are single and living it up with no intention of settling down anytime soon, you should prepare yourself to wait for commitment—and if you're not willing to wait, you might need to move on. Why? Well, it takes a strong man to break out from his friends and be the first to commit. However, that is not to say that your guy couldn't be the first one to take the plunge. Just know that it will take much more effort to get him there.

So in the all-his-friends-are-single situation, what kind of man should you consider gambling your heart on? The answer is the *responsive* one. What do we mean by responsive? Let us explain.

Picture a group of four guys shooting the breeze and chatting at happy hour. One guy says, "I was talking to Bob about stashing away money for retirement as a percentage of his income and he tells me he doesn't really keep track of how much he makes. Can you imagine that?" One of the other guys says, "Yeah, Bob's a space cadet. He doesn't even know how much he makes!" The third guy echoes those sentiments. The fourth guy, however, actually doesn't keep track of his income either—what will he do? He could nod and echo the others' sentiments, or keep quiet, but instead he speaks up and says, "You know, I don't think that Bob has an issue at all. In fact, I don't keep track of my income either."

Which guy is the one who might be most likely to commit? In spite of not keeping track of his income, we'd put our money on bachelor number four. Why? Because he wasn't afraid to differentiate himself from the pack even if it meant looking foolish or causing dissension. He is *responsive*. He is not pressured by the group, and therefore likely the most mature. And a guy who has a strong sense of "I" is going to be more able to commit to becoming a "We" without fear of losing himself in the process.

Basically, men and women (we're not letting you totally off the hook) who are less mature—which also means less likely to differentiate themselves from their friends—often find that they are more *reactive* than *responsive* when challenged. Reactive means that they're likely to get defensive and disproportionately emotional. Accordingly, reactive responses usually show up when a person feels emotionally threatened or provoked. The question to consider when figuring out your guy's ability to differentiate from his pack is this: How often and what triggers his emotion-driven reaction?

For example, what happens if you bring up some commit-ment-related issues? This could be a very emotionally pre-carious topic for your man. If he's vulnera-phobic at all, his comeback will likely be reactive (*Help! She's attacking me!*). If your guy says anything like "Why do we have to keep dis-cussing this? You know I am into you. Don't you trust me?" or perhaps "If you believed in our relationship, you would be able to stop pressing me for more," he's reacting reflexively and defensively. In other words, he's not addressing the issue, he's feeling bombarded, and he might even try to deflect the issue back to you (for example, "It's your problem that you're feeling insecure about our commitment, not mine"). And not surprisingly, his defensiveness will probably make you feel even more insecure than you already were about the direction the relationship is heading.

The opposite of being reactive is being responsive. When a person is responsive he is not reacting reflexively. Such people are aware of their feelings but don't let them take over. This is extremely empowering. Responsiveness allows a guy (or a woman, of course) to maintain some control in the face of conflicting thoughts and feelings of significant others. The mature guy, not run by his feelings, will find him-self enjoying all sorts of new options and choices in his deal-ings with others because his perspective and sense of reason aren't being blurred by emotion. This will allow him to feel more in control, which is a good thing since a less-reactive man is a better bet when it comes to commitment potential. Why? The responsive man is in a better position to take con-trol of his love life—and he won't flip into vulnera-phobia mode at the drop of a hat for fear that he will lose himself to a woman. He is secure with who he is, so he is capable of going against what his peers say or do, and he is able to entertain the idea of commitment with a woman without panic. But perhaps most importantly, he has come to accept that a certain degree of vulnerability doesn't make him less of a man, but rather it makes him a more complete one.

Of course, becoming responsive is easier said than done since behavioral changes are a struggle for everyone. In essence it requires identifying with what it is that you want, believe, or feel and staying the course. It also involves being open to views that are in conflict with your own rather than getting defensive. That means when talking to someone who disagrees with you, for example, instead of arguing, explaining yourself, or apologizing, you might simply say, "You're entitled to your opinion." Another good answer would be, "That's interesting," or "Let me think about that," rather than an anger reaction. If you catch your man responding to your queries in this sort of manner, you may have a keeper. He is exhibiting the behavior of someone willing to step up to the plate and someone who isn't afraid to consider opinions that differ from his.

Bottom line: He's secure with who he is, and a secure man is always a better bet when it comes to commitment potential. In fact, the irony to keep in mind is that a man who has a good sense of separateness (a solid "I") has a greater capacity for and less fear of intimacy (a greater chance of forming a committed "We").

When you are assessing a guy's reactivity or responsiveness, also consider if you are enabling his behavior by being a pathological empathic (yes, that again!). It's easy, however, to make excuses for your guy when he gets defensive or to think, "It must have been something I said" or "If only I had phrased that differently, it might have gone better." Stop letting him off the hook! If you're dealing with a mature man, you're not going to have to keep trying to explain away his inability to commit or deal with your differences.

Meeting the Chick Clique

Another important thing to consider in this section is does he care to meet *your* friends? Remember, this is about integrating both of your lives. If the man you're dating shows no interest in meeting anyone who you call near and dear, you should be worried—unless you're planning on ditching all your friends (which we do *not* recommend because if the relationship doesn't work out it's your friends who you'll be leaning on, not your ex). He needs to be open to joining in on an activity that includes your friends. Will it be scary for him? You bet! He knows he's being judged by the ultimate panel, but if you're more than a fling, if you're really the real thing to him, he's going to welcome the challenge.

Another method you can use to discern your guy's commitment-mindedness is to see how he reacts to a mention of your platonic male friends. Any man who is thinking future with you is probably not going to be all that happy about you having a close friendship with another guy. If your male friend is heterosexual, your boyfriend won't be able to stop himself from considering the possibility that any other guy is probably going to be just like him in thinking, *I'd like to have sex with her!*

This example of healthy jealousy may actually indicate that your guy is in this relationship for real. How so? If he really loves you, the idea that this love may possibly be lost to someone else is a threat. He doesn't want to lose you. He's invested. He's into you (at least for now—it doesn't mean it will last, but it's a good sign that there is an attachment forming).

One thing to keep in mind, however, is that this does not include irrational jealousy—for example, if your boss buys you a gift for pulling an all-nighter to finish a huge project and your guy freaks out. That sort of thing is just unwarranted.

But if he gets a little jealous when one of your guy friends gives you attention, then go ahead and smile, because your man is definitely showing a positive commitment sign.

Commitment and Family

Once you've met someone you adore, you may think that your relationship with him is the most important one you have to work on. But don't forget, your man is only a sum of his parts, and that includes his family. Like it or not, your interactions with his mom, dad, siblings, and other relatives can actually have a huge impact on your relationship with your partner. But even more than that, his introduction of you to his family can give you a myriad of clues as to where your relationship is heading.

Sometimes in a relationship's progression, there are actual circumstances preventing him from easily taking you home, like his parents fight all the time, his mother drinks too much, or his family lives across the country. More often, however, a hesitancy to share you with his nearest and dearest is actually him saying "No commitment here," and you not hearing it.

Even before a trip to meet the family though, you can glean another big clue about his commitment intentions from his mentions of you to them. In other words, does his family know you exist? If he hasn't discussed you with his parents or siblings, you are not yet beyond some-girl-I'm-dating status. A man inherently knows that his family wants him to settle down and be happy, and he's not going to risk letting them get attached to a woman if he doesn't think that there is at least the possibility of something more than a fling developing.

And much of this is also predicated on his relationship with his family, of course. Some men don't share much with their parents (then again, some men don't share much at all, but we'll get to that later). Whatever the case, it does seem that a man's relationship with and within his family structure can also shed light on the way he might function within a romantic coupling.

If you do make it to the meeting-the-family phase, don't assume that means you're bound for easy acceptance. Occasionally that may be the case. Sometimes you may even fall harder for his family than you have for the guy (which makes it tough if the relationship doesn't pan out, because then you have to break up with him and his family). But even if you aren't immediately seen as one of them, your interactions with his various family members will be telling of your relationship with him.

Is He More like Mom or Dad?

One thing you should pay attention to is who is the dominant member of the family (are you dealing with a matriarch or patriarch?). The power head is often very influential. You can either ask him outright for the answer or ascertain by your own observations who wears the pants. Then notice how your guy deals with this distribution of power. It will be very telling.

Most relationships have a more dominant and a more submissive person. If the family has a strong mother, for example, the father is usually more submissive, accommodating. Who is your boyfriend more similar to in temperament? If he is more like his mother, more dominant, he will be attracted to someone more submissive, like his father. Do you fit that role? This is just another thing to take into consideration when looking at the long-term viability of your relationship. If you are both dominant personalities or both submissive personalities, one of you may have to back off or step up in order to make things work. If that doesn't happen, things may eventually disintegrate between the two of you. There has to be a power exchange in order for things to run smoothly. And sometimes, it might switch (for example, you might be more dominant in some situations and then at other times more accommodating).

Another thing to keep in mind is that if your man is more submissive and you are more dominant—which is usually how it works if that is his personality—you may eventually clash with your dominant counterpart in his family. And quarrels between a partner and one's family are never an easy thing for a couple to work through if they have long-term commitment on the agenda. Bear in mind, like it or not, commitment comes as a package deal—your man plus his family.

You also want to consider how his father treats his mother. His father, especially if he is a strong figure, is the model that your guy has been influenced by and sooner or later, for better or worse, you are likely to see the image of the father appear in the son's behavior. Learned behaviors are deep-seated and even if your beau is not aware of their influence, he has been affected one way or another by what he's seen growing up.

But don't think that means your guy will end up exactly like his dad. In fact, a more telling indicator of how he will behave in a romantic relationship is not the interaction between his parents but rather his own personal relationship *with* his parents. Support for this theory emanates from a study done at Iowa State University's Institute for Social and Behavioral Research. Based on observations made by trained investigators who spent time observing the families that participated in this study, the research, which spanned an eleven-year period, also included family surveys and videotaped interactions between adolescents, siblings, and parents. The researchers observed the children in these families from age twelve and up. Then years later, the researchers observed 193 of the same children who were now in their twenties and in ongoing romantic relationships.

The results? Adolescents who grew up with parents who were warm and understanding toward them tended to develop similar relationships with their romantic partners. The situation was reversed if children grew up in families that were not supportive. Those children tended to have unstable and unhappy relationships as adults. The results also suggest that children from single-parent families may do just as well as those from two-parent families in romantic relationships, as long as they have equally supportive parents.

Bottom line: Parenting has a major impact on an individual's future relationships, independent of the quality of the parents' marriage. Good parenting, even in marriages that struggle or have ended in divorce, increases the probability that the offspring will do better in their adult romantic relationships.

So, do these findings and family dynamics mean you should discard any guy who has an iffy or less than an ideal relationship with his parents? Heck no! We're not saying that. We're just presenting this info because it could mean you will face tougher challenges if you get involved with a guy who actively expresses a disconnect with his parents in some way or mentions that they were not there for him in the way he wishes they had been when he was growing up. But keep in mind that counseling can always help when these types of barriers are hit if the relationship is worth working for, and if your guy is open to it—which may be an entirely different issue in and of itself.

Changing Primary Allegiance

Notice how he is treated within the context of his family. Some guys have a difficult time making the transition from family of origin to new family. This may especially be the case in some Mediterranean groups like Greeks and Italians, and in many Jewish sects. The boys in these cultures are sometimes treated like royalty and there may be some resentment within his family that you are "taking him away." What's more, he may have difficulty or even feel a conflict of loyalty breaking away from Momma. In actuality it doesn't have to be a "breaking away" but more a degree of separation that allows commitment and intimacy with his woman. But if your man is not open to that separation or is clearly bending to the will of his family, it may make him a more difficult commitment prospect for you.

Any relationship is going to have its challenges, but if you're lucky, fitting into his family won't be an issue. Once again, however, you should also look at how he relates to *your* family. If you're the one dealing with abandonment issues or struggling with a dysfunctional family, you may be the one who has to do some of the healing self-help work to make the relationship gel. An important sign, however, is if your man is willing to hang in there with you no matter what your family situation. If the going gets tough and he checks out, then that's not a partner you want. Remember, you're looking for someone who is in it for better or for worse here. Find the guy who is going to fight to stay in your corner. The guy who has a history of working things out, not quitting, unless quitting is the thing to do.

Commitment Is Openness

When it comes to finding a partner whom you can love and trust, it is important to establish a degree of openness with the man in your life. But, this may be easier said than done. To begin with, getting a man to share his innermost thoughts can act as a direct trigger to his vulnera-phobia. He might think, *Oh no, she wants to "know" me now and then if she finds out all about me, she might not like me anymore or she'll know too much about me if we don't work out and . . . I'd better be guarded.* Seriously, you can see it on their faces as soon as you start trying to get closer.

Some of this may come from past experience; for example, he was judged harshly by a previous girlfriend and doesn't want to re-experience that pain. Or perhaps he anticipates that sharing will cause him future hurt because of the war he saw going on between his own parents his whole life. And there is also the possibility that some guys have never learned what real openness is truly about; they may not have had a family model for openness.

Whatever the case, being guarded has become a natural state for many guys (and to be fair, many women as well). It's a scary and vulnerable thing to open up to another person. As a result—whether consciously or not—people often tend to camouflage their true selves as protection against criticism or rejection. The protection, however, comes at a steep price. Being too guarded can keep a relationship from flourishing, and it can definitely prevent a couple from integrating their lives and moving toward commitment. Why? Well, how can you learn to trust each other and build a bond of intimacy if you're constantly keeping secrets from one another and possibly from yourselves as well?

Openness and learning to share is one of the foundations of a healthy relationship where a couple learns to grow together, as a unit. And of course, that trust can also be a sign of maturity and a willingness to be a little vulnerable in order to get closer—a good sign of commitment potential.

To get a sense of your guy's share-ability, try taking this openness quiz we've created. Keep in mind that although this is not a precise scientific instrument (a brief scale can't capture all of the nuances involved, and you're projecting what he would answer), it will give you a better idea whether you're really getting to know the man you're with, or if there may be more work to do in order to uncover his true colors.

OPENNESS QUIZ

So here's the deal. Grab a pen and number a piece of paper from one to ten. Read each scenario below and indicate how well it applies to your man's self-disclosure behavior (as best you can) using the following point system we've outlined. When you get to the end, add up the numbers and you'll have his projected openness score.

Zero points = No way!
One point = Um…maybe?
Two Points = There is a good chance.
Three Points = Pretty much for sure.

1. You and your beau are reading the Sunday paper together over brunch. There is an Op/Ed about a controversial subject like abortion rights or the death penalty and you state your position very strongly after scanning the

piece. Your man realizes that he takes the totally opposite stance. He could stay quiet and keep the Sunday peace, or he could let you know his alternate views on the subject. How likely is it that he will share his opinion with you, even at the risk of a heated debate?

2. You know that your guy has dated a lot of women but you don't know the details. One day you are in the grocery store together when he suddenly pulls you in the other direction to hide from some lady coming the other way down the aisle. You guess correctly that this was an ex-girlfriend—and from his behavior can clearly tell things didn't end well. You ask your guy for the lowdown. How likely is it that he will share the nitty-gritty about what happened to end the relationship (even if it was his fault)?

3. When it comes to kids, you know you want a family but you are afraid to bring it up for fear of scaring off your boyfriend. However, one day you two end up babysitting for your cousin's three-year-old girl. After hours at the playground, you jokingly say, "Wow, I guess this is what it would be like if we had a little one." How likely is it that your boyfriend will pick up on the underlying message in your suggestive statement and enter a discussion about his desire to have kids?

4. Your sex life with your man has been terrific and balanced for months, but recently he's more often than not been pushing things out of your comfort zone, like having rougher and more disconnected sex even though you prefer sensual sex. You decide to mention this sexual shift one night at dinner. How likely is it that your man

will calmly discuss his feelings about this in an effort to find middle ground?

5. You know that you and your guy come from different religious backgrounds. It is important to your family that he convert if you are to stay together, though it's not as big a deal to you. However, you decide to bring the issue to the table to see if he would be open to the change one day if it were necessary to get your parents' consent for a committed relationship. How likely is it that he would be open-minded to this type of discussion?

6. You and your guy meet his good friend and respective girlfriend for a double date. During dinner the conversation is lagging so you decide to pick up the slack by sharing funny stories of things you and your boyfriend have done recently, but in so doing, you inadvertently embarrass him by sharing some things that he considers private. He could sulk and say nothing about the incident, or he could mention that he thought you offered up too many intimate details and he felt hurt. How likely is it that he will bring this up later?

7. You are headed out of town for an important conference for work and it is the first time you'll be away from each other since you two started dating. Your guy suddenly gets really moody before you leave and you can't figure out what's wrong. Turns out that he had a past girlfriend cheat on him while on a business trip and he's feeling nervous that the same thing will happen, though inherently he knows you're not his ex and history doesn't necessarily repeat itself. How likely is it that he will share this fear with you?

8. Your boyfriend has a dog that he adores but lately it's been misbehaving by getting into the trash, peeing on the floor, and whining during the night so you can't sleep when you're over (though *he* sleeps through it). Amazingly, he doesn't seem to see it as a big problem, but you recognize that if you're going to stay together for the long term it is going to frustrate and upset you if not addressed. Finally, you dare to bring up the dog issue even though you know it's a sensitive subject. Will he listen to your concerns and try to come up with an equitable solution that accommodates both you and the dog?

9. You know that your boyfriend and his best friend from childhood recently had a serious falling out and they don't really speak anymore, but you don't know the reason behind the disagreement. You can tell, however, that he still hurts when he mentions his friend's name in conjunction with a memory or place they went together. One day you ask him what happened. How likely is it that he will give you the whole story?

10. It's easy to sometimes think only of the here and now when you are in the throes of a new relationship, but as things start to move forward, you need to figure out if your goals as a couple line up. You have a bunch of questions: Do you want to live in the city/country? Do you plan to keep working even if you have kids? Would he be okay with you not working if you started a family? Could you live off one salary? Where do you see yourself in twenty years? This kind of "future" talk can be frightening for a guy, but it is also vital if you're thinking commitment. How likely is it that he will engage you in a discussion involving these issues?

The Results

Okay, time to add up his points. The total should range from zero to thirty. If the score is relatively high, it looks like you think your guy is being fairly open with you. If the score is on the low side, he may still be a little guarded. But don't think that all is lost and that the relationship is totally dysfunctional if he's not sporting top numbers. It just might mean that there is a little more work to be done to break down the barriers. Still, here is a more detailed account of where your guy might fall on the openness scale.

The Guarded Guy (0–10 points)

It is highly likely that your beau is still very careful about what he tells you at this point. Most likely it's a fear of getting too close that keeps him from sharing his deepest thoughts, secrets, and desires (read: *vulnera-phobia in high gear*). But whether he knows he's doing this or not, until he opens up a little, it will be very difficult for you two to continue to grow as a couple. While he might convince himself that he's not telling you about his past indiscretions and history to protect you, it's much more likely that he's not divulging in order to protect himself from hurt or possible rejection. Though there is certainly no reason he has to tell you everything, if commitment is truly the goal, he will eventually need to learn to share some of himself with you or your relationship will always be shrouded with an air of secrecy.

The Safe Sharer (11–20 points)

If your guy scores in this category, it indicates that getting closer to you is something he might actually desire, but he's also still really nervous about exposing too much of himself. This may come from past experience (for example, he shared too much in the past with a woman and it came back to bite him later), or it might be that he doesn't know how much of himself he can share without feeling like he might scare you off. In other words, he's afraid that if you know the real him you may leave. The fear of abandonment or rejection can run very strongly in men, especially ones who have loved and lost before (either romantically or otherwise). However, intimacy between two people truly begins when both partners feel safe sharing anything and everything with each other. The good news is that this guy may just need a little coaxing to open up more but the instinct is there. Consider starting small by asking him to divulge stories about his childhood or challenging him to remember the best day of his life so far. As he gets more comfortable with sharing his past, it may encourage more openness in his present.

The Committed Confidant (21–30 points)

If you scored your guy fairly high, you two could be on your way to a truly open relationship. This is a good sign for commitment potential because the average dude is not going to risk sharing his emotions with any random chick. The potential to lose face is too high if they aren't invested in the relationship—most men would rather be tortured than experience vulnerability. However, once a man recognizes that being honest with his woman will actually allow him to grow closer to her, he will also be on his way toward entertaining the idea of a future together. It's about taking a chance, and it's likely that the more mature and solid guy will risk feeling foolish by divulging his innermost thoughts. Openness is vital to a healthy relationship that has potential for the long haul. The good news for you? A man scoring solidly in this category is likely coming to understand the benefits of being part of a happy, committed couple.

Viva la Difference

Okay, so now that you've determined where your guy may fall on the openness scale, there is one more critical component to consider, which is that, by nature, men and women tend to share differently. And this becomes extremely obvious in the context of an amorous relationship. One big issue that we alluded to in the previous quiz, for example, is what's considered private and what's not. Women are so used to sharing everything that they are very liberal with what they consider *too much* to tell their best gal pals. Guys, on the other hand, may consider any discussions with other guys about their sex life, relationship issues, or even their quirks (which you think are cute but he might perceive as weaknesses in his character) totally off-limits. And, for some men, it doesn't matter which one is sharing the details—even *listening* to his pal's confession may be uncomfortable. This difference in the definition of openness for the sexes can definitely lead to miscommunications and couple meltdowns.

Men are not only cautious with one another; they are also more hesitant to communicate intimately with the women in their lives, especially before they feel emotionally safe. Remember our previous discussion about men's actions taking precedence over their words? Same deal here. Men are typically much more comfortable acting on something rather than talking about something. This may lead to another disconnect between the sexes when a woman thinks her guy is withholding stuff from her when actually he thinks he's sharing more than enough through his actions. On the flip side, a man may judge a woman predicated on what she does rather than what she says. See where we're going with this?

You need to keep in mind that men and women have different expectations of what openness means. Therefore, a guy may think you're in an intimate relationship if you know exactly how he takes his Starbucks latte. Women, on the other hand, tend to want a lot more sharing than that in a committed relationship. She may want to really *know* him, while he's desperately trying to figure out how to keep a little space. Keep in mind, men also fear losing themselves by entering into intimate relationships.

Additionally, women and men frequently work out differences differently. Men, on the whole, tend to be less in touch with their feelings. Of course, there are exceptions, but by nature women just tend to be the more emotional sex. Guys are also frequently afraid that expressing their emotions isn't manly or they fear they will become overwhelmed and lose control. Women, however, are better able to handle intense feelings if they are openly expressed. It is withdrawal and underlying rage from their partner that disturbs them the most because they want and need communication. You know what we're talking about. A clear example is when a woman says, "What are you thinking? You seem upset" and her guy snaps, "Nothing. I'm fine." He doesn't want to share, but she needs to know what's going on. There's an openness disconnect in full effect.

So, does this mean that openness differences between the sexes doom all relationships to eternal secret keeping? Not necessarily. The closer you get as a couple, the less important it will become for either one of you to hide things from each other. It's about building trust and a safe zone in which sharing becomes natural.

If the desire to increase the openness between you two is approached in a nonthreatening, sensitive manner, you are much more likely to get cooperation, if not fully, at least partially. One easy way to encourage this, no matter where you are in your relationship, is to lead by example. Don't be afraid to make the first move to reach out and share with him. Inherently, men (and women) show more understanding and compassion when on the receiving end of openness. The irony is that men, who usually view their vulnerability as kryptonite, often find a woman's openness—as long is it isn't over the top—as connective. While he may guard his own privacy, a degree of openness on his partner's side is actually welcome.

However, there's no guarantee that acting open with your guy will produce positive results. But you have a far greater chance of getting him to reciprocate than if you do nothing or clam up. Think of it this way: You are creating an environment in which you two can learn to share. If he doesn't take the bait, well then at least you can feel good about having learned to reveal your inner thoughts. It takes guts to be open with another person and if you're up to the challenge then you're showing enough maturity to handle commitment, which is definitely part of this equation. Remember, it takes two people to commit, and sometimes women aren't there yet either.

Consider carefully where both you and your partner are in the commitment process—as well as the goal of your relationship—before giving your heart away. No matter how much you may think you want a relationship, unless you are both fully invested and truly available to commit, the prospects for longevity will be diminished—but we'll discuss that more in the next chapter.

The important thing to keep in mind here is that thoughtfulness in a committed relationship includes sharing your lives and fostering honesty and openness. And yes, it does need to be reciprocal for long-term survival. If you are the only one opening your heart and your life, ultimately, you will be left unfulfilled.

THE COMMITMENT-READY MAN ... Is primed to meet your friends and family, and to introduce you to his because he's proud to have you in his life and wants to show you off. He realizes that he's less vulnerable with you at his side because you're part of a team. And he's willing to share his thoughts and hopes with you because he recognizes the trust you've built as a unit. He'll find security, not threat, in your integrated lives.

8

COMMITMENT
Means Being Available to Commit

*B*ut *he really loves me; I know he does. He's just not in a place to be able to commit right now, but as soon as he is free again, I'll be the one—without a doubt. I'm sure of it.* Sound familiar? It's the little voice in the female head that convinces herself somehow, some way, the man she's seeing who is technically, emotionally, or otherwise unavailable to commit fully at this moment in time will magically transform into a ready-to-wed male version as soon as he deals with his "stuff."

What kind of stuff are we referring to? Well, it could be a wife he's in the process of separating from, or he might be just out of a serious relationship, or have issues that make him emotionally unavailable, or be dealing with a compulsion or addiction—the list goes on and on.

The problem with that little voice women hear? It allows an unavailable man (who might also be a vulnera-phobic man) to string along a woman much longer than should be permissible. Not to mention the fact that it turns a woman into a pathological empathic who makes excuses for him over and over and over again.

Dating a man who is actually unavailable to commit adds yet another layer to the omnipresent vulnera-phobia threat. How so? Well, even if this male wants to commit or tells you he wants to, he can't (whether legally or psychologically). For this reason, certain relationships, or rather certain situations within relationships in which many women find themselves embroiled, can make for very iffy commitment gambles.

We're not trying to make things sound totally dire, but the reality is the odds are not usually very good for future longevity when starting from one of these scenarios. Sure, on occasion it works out, but it's not the norm. And since we've spent most of this book trying to help you stack the odds in your favor for commitment, it would be wrong of us not to point out the importance of an availability to commit in the commitment equation—for him, for you, for the long-term success of your relationship.

The Married Man Mess

There's more than one little hitch with dating a man who's, well, hitched. In fact, the issues go well beyond the fact that he already has a wife. Many women convince themselves that a relationship with an unhappily married man is okay because if the marriage actually mattered, he wouldn't feel a need to stray. So, they assume they're not playing the role of home-wrecker; they're just sweeping in before it's a total wreck so that when things *do* fall apart completely, they'll be there to pick up the diamond ring and run with this man toward a happy future.

Time for a reality check though. In most of the cases where a woman has an affair with a married man, when and if the marriage does finally end and reality sets in, the woman waiting in the wings to step out of the understudy role and into the leading part in this man's life isn't the one who he eventually ends up with (if he remarries at all). In fact, in talking to a myriad of married men who'd had affairs, we discovered that only about one out of ten had married, or were about to marry, the person with whom they were having an affair. This isn't surprising when you factor in that only about twenty percent of the divorces were sought in order to marry the adulteress; even when they were, the planned remarriages took place only about half the time—the divorce process brings a reality to an affair that rattles even the hardiest of lovers.

For one thing, an affair resembles courtship and divorce alters this. During the affair, lovers limit themselves to a narrow behavioral and social repertoire aimed at pleasing each other. Often this repertoire consists of precisely the kind of behavior lacking at home. In addition, there is the excitement of "lovers against the world"—the clandestine adventure includes secret trips, sojourns at hotels under false names, and so on.

Their emotional investment in these risks convinces the lovers that the affair is the high point of their lives. With the divorce, the drama calms down, and while the strains of secrecy and jealousy are removed, new ones are introduced. For example, the divorcing lover may cop out after being exposed to unpalatable divorce-battle behavior—his depleted finances, emotional outbursts, vindictiveness—all of which have a dampening effect on his new romance. Now the lovers really get to know each other and some of the revelations may be totally unexpected if not shocking. In fact, the dynamics of the newly formulated relationship may barely resemble the fantasy experience of the affair.

. . . .

Reality Bites

To further explain this point about the shifting dynamic once an extramarital relationship is no longer secret (and consequently exciting), consider Jonathan, a thirty-eight-year-old engineer who'd had an affair with a woman named Helen prior to the end of his marriage.

After separating from my wife, I moved in with my mistress, Helen. For the first time in our two-year relationship, we were able to assume the legitimate roles of lovers. It seemed like things were finally going to be the way we had hoped, but almost immediately conflict erupted.

Helen demanded that I be more attentive now that we were legitimately together. In the past, she had understood my difficulty in seeing her—I was married. Now, she insisted there was no excuse. If I worked late, she became upset. If I was tied up in my job for several days in a row, she was irritated, resentful, and openly antagonistic. Seeing this side of Helen, I began to have serious misgivings about marriage, although I had felt certain for months that I wanted to marry her. Helen, sensing my withdrawal, felt frightened and betrayed. As a result, she became more antagonistic and on many mornings provoked an argument just before I left for the office. I began to work even later, and Helen felt more left out than ever. The cycle lasted six weeks; the new marriage, conceived in idealism, died unborn.

. . . .

Jonathan's situation is not uncommon, unfortunately. During the affair phase, things seem ideal, perfect even. But that's because it's not reality. Both partners are able to give only the best of themselves to the relationship thanks to the fact that their time together is borrowed. They come together for a brief, explosive union. It's all chemistry and intrigue, and then they go about their own lives. While they're together there is none of the chore-sharing or bill-paying daily drama that real-life couples must be able to negotiate together. Think of it like this: If a real committed relationship is a team, an affair is the fantasy league version.

Mistress Misery

Another thing to keep in mind with this fool's paradise aspect of an extramarital affair is the state of mind you would have to be in to agree to enter into such a relationship. We're not accusing here and we know accidents happen, like he wasn't wearing a ring and the marital status was kept hidden until the woman put the pieces together, but frequently a woman goes into a married affair with her eyes wide open. Why would a commitment-minded woman do this? Well, if commitment is really the goal, she shouldn't.

That said, sometimes a woman might find herself feeling lonely or depressed about her single status and then meets a married man who is handsome, financially stable, and, best of all, into her. Suddenly, her life looks a little more interesting. There is intrigue, there is passion, there is the possibility of sex, there is a little bit of excitement, and there is the thrill of doing something forbidden. And if the woman can keep her heart out of it, it might work—at least for a while. But usually someone in such a low enough state of mind to enter into an affair is not going to stay detached. She's going to start pinning her hopes on the affair turning into something more. Why? Well, for one thing, the affair is so crazily stimulating that it's like a drug, so for a while this woman is lifted out of her depression and enabled to feel things again. And she starts to like it, to cling to it, to remember what love is like.

Of course, it doesn't last, because between moments of ecstasy, she will then become even more depressed than she was initially and feel increasingly alone and unnaturally hooked on the affair partner (because he becomes the "dealer" for making her feel good again). See the vicious cycle that's emerging? What this woman is forgetting in the process as well is that there is another woman still very much in the picture and unless threesomes are a thing for all parties involved, the possibility of heartbreak is huge for any woman diving into a serious relationship with a married man.

....

Married Man Magnets

Sadly for Marie, her situation is case in point:

I met Hank at a business function almost two years ago. He's forty-eight and I am thirty-four. He wasn't wearing a wedding band but he told me he was still legally married until his divorce became finalized. He didn't say when that would be. At first our conversations were focused on our common business interests, but I knew there was something more, and it was obvious he did as well. First, there were the lunches, then drinks after work. Then more drinks and lingering, and then we ended up at my place. That's how it started and now it's become even more intense. We both travel extensively for business and we arrange to meet when we are both out of town—not some of the time, but all of the time.

The sex is hotter than either of us have ever experienced. We literally spend days in bed. I mean it is really intense. And it's not all about sex. Our conversations are charged. It's like an electrical current between us. Those are the good parts, the things that keep me hooked—that and the promise that we have a future together.

The bad part, and it is really bad, is that I don't believe him anymore. I've given him nearly two years and what he describes as his "divorce in process" seems not to be what he said it was. At best, it's a far-off goal; at worst, it's a line. My dilemma is this: As crazy as it is—and I know it's crazy—I am in love with him. I also have been growing more and more scared that my fertility years are flying by. I know what I should do, but every time I hear his voice or see him, I get drawn in.

What Marie is experiencing is one of the craziest and most destructive forms of hope. It is the temporary insanity of falling in love with a married guy. It's one thing to have a physical affair; it's quite another to engage in an affair of the heart. And remember, it's not okay to just say, "Well, he was wonderful, I couldn't help it." Wonderful people don't screw around on their partners (and lie about their "real" status to you as well).

....

We assume that if you're reading this book, you are seemingly interested in finding someone truly wonderful and commitment-minded. *But if a man is married, it means he's not afraid of making a commitment to a woman,* you may think. Good try, but we don't buy that train of thought. Just because a guy has committed before doesn't mean he'll necessarily do it again—or that he'll ever commit to you.

We concede that it does occasionally work out for some people. And if a marriage is broken by an affair and the lovers marry, it is then assumed that the original marriage was unhappy and that the illicit transgression was sincere. The affair becomes legitimized by the marriage, and the couple re-enters society together. This is the idealized version. In actual life, it is a rarity.

The Marriage Mirage

To keep things in perspective, you need to realize that most relationships that start as affairs do not end up with the man leaving his wife and marrying the mistress. Romantic affairs may lead to divorces, suicides, homicides, and broken hearts, but not to very many successful remarriages. The more typical scenario is that no matter how many sacrifices the woman may make to keep the love alive, it will gradually burn itself out when there is nothing more to sacrifice to it. Then she must face not only the wreckage of lives, but also the original depression from which she was trying to escape with the affair.

Another really important part of this equation to consider as well is the desire for children. If having babies is a goal, spending time in a relationship with a married man is likely eating up some of your possible childbearing years with no guarantee of a commitment down the road. And even if this married man does finally make the move to be with you, think about the time required for him to extricate himself from the other relationship.

In other words, are you ready to wait for your married lover to make up his mind to leave his wife, get the ball rolling, tell her he's ending the marriage, work on getting the divorce, wait for the divorce to go through, wait an appropriate amount of time after the divorce is final before getting engaged again, spend time with you as a real couple before planning the wedding, and then . . . see where we're going with this? Our guess is that most women involved in an affair with a married man don't want to wait that long but they aren't thinking realistically about the timeline involved in ending a marriage in order to move into another one. And chances are her clock is ticking a lot faster than his.

But he really loves me too so I know this will happen . . . eventually. Okay, you know what? Maybe he does love you. But keep in mind this is likely a different kind of love than the long-term "I want to marry you and have you bear my children" kind of love. Remember, he's already got steady love at home (even if he says it's dysfunctional, it's still there) and, in case you hadn't noticed, you don't. So who does that make the more vulnerable person in this equation? That's right. It's you.

Men in affairs are not likely to experience the vulnera-phobia they might if they weren't otherwise entangled, because at this point, there is no need for them to feel it. You might press them for a bigger commitment, but as long as they're technically married, they have a safety net. So they feel free to love you, enjoy you, get close to you, but because the pressure to immediately commit to you isn't there, they're not as likely to run. Keep in mind as well that men in love often lose their heads—at least for a while. Frequently, somewhere down the line in an affair, however, things change. The man becomes guilt-ridden and reluctant to completely leave a marriage he has betrayed and even deserted. His lover is left hopeful for a wedding in the future, but that is not likely to happen.

Unfortunately all this means that some women get stuck in relationships with married men for years. How so? Well, a woman can keep clinging to the idea that her married lover will leave his wife to be with her indefinitely as long as he reassures her that will eventually be the case. Once again, however, we must point out—it's all about his actions. If he's not doing it, then he's not committed to the idea, and in fact, might be perfectly fine with the wife/mistress dual life.

Another thing to consider? Even if he does make a move toward severing his first marriage, guys who jump immediately from one marriage to another, even if preceded by a long-term affair, are high-risk prospects for commitment. At a time of emotional weariness from the divorce process, he is not likely to exercise sound judgment. If he commits, he is likely to have second thoughts. If he has lived alone for a time, the odds that he's for real and serious about commitment are higher but still nowhere near a guarantee.

That said, it's important to also realize that although it's difficult to get really precise numbers, research and clinical observations suggest that just over one-third of affairs that lead to marriage work out well, while the nearly two-thirds remaining fail—a failure rate decidedly higher than that of the first marriage divorce rate.

This may indicate that there is something about the illicit origin of such marriages that dooms them. In a fair number of cases, there does seem to be a special kind of marital problem or cluster of problems that relates to the way the relationship began. But when one looks more closely, another factor may be present—there may have been pre-existing psychological issues in one or both persons, or in their relationship with each other.

What factors? The guy may have a sense of guilt toward his rejected wife, which is directed toward his present partner, his new wife, or his live-in lover. Or perhaps patterns that undermine relationships, which went undetected during the affair, emerge in the new marriage. Then there is the aforementioned loss of excitement that the clandestine nature of the affair had provided. And there may be other emotions or conditions that the new union was not prepared to handle because the foundation on which it started was already mired with complications.

Misguided Trust

If all of the previous scenarios haven't yet convinced you that dating a married man might not be your best move if commitment is your goal, please consider the following:

1. He's cheating on her; he's likely to cheat on you.
2. You are not getting to know the *real* him.
3. He's a liar and has a flawed character.
4. You're going to be a bit player in his next soap opera, like if he and his wife do split, you could be pulled into the mess.
5. He'll have plenty of excuses for why he is staying married to his wife, but none of those excuses are truthful—he's married to someone else because he wants to be.
6. If he actually leaves his wife, which he most likely won't, he's not likely to marry you, and if he does, your relationship is likely to fail.

Bottom line: Influenced by passion, consumed by hope, giddy with love, we would suggest that any commitment-minded woman who is tempted to get involved with a married guy, or even a guy who says he is recently separated, would do better to stop, think, and at the very least *wait*.

Flirting with Disaster

The disaster to which we refer here is a "he," not an event. It's the emotionally unavailable man, who also might be *technically* unavailable, as in married—but since we've just covered that, we're going to assume this man is "otherwise" unavailable. We're talking about the man who thinks he wants a committed relationship or says he's ready for another serious relationship (if he's been in one before) but doesn't realize that thinking and doing are two *very* different animals. This could also include the man who is so wrapped up in other things outside of his romantic relationship that he's unable to be truly available for his partner in the way he needs to be for a committed relationship to work.

Sometimes, the most convincing guy is the one who doesn't even know that he's incapable of handling intimacy or that he has issues preventing him from truly being "in" a relationship; denial is a very powerful mind trick. In any case, the thing to remember is that while flirting with Disaster may be very tempting and even appealing, he is also a very poor commitment prospect.

When it comes to the various forms Disaster may take, there are several that really come into play (and sadly we can imagine that you may have encountered a few others that are not even on this list). In order to prep you for finding out if your man's ready to commit, let's take a look at a few higher-risk males that are in no way ready to do so.

Mr. Just-Broke-Up-With-My-Serious-Girlfriend

Technically, this guy sounds available. He's not with someone, he's on the market, he seems to be looking (we're assuming because you just met him somehow), but is he *really* ready for another relationship? Or is he licking his wounds and trying to make himself feel better again because she dumped him?

Conversely, if it was the other way around and he dumped her, shouldn't he *still* be waiting a bit to figure out what it is he really wants before dragging some other girl's heart into the mix? In other words, wouldn't it be wiser to let him regroup, rather than appoint you as his transitional lover? Well, we would like to think so, but many guys don't look at it that way. Men tend to run from their feelings unless they've had their heart shattered, so he will not confront his feelings unless he's forced.

Keep in mind that women take much longer than men to heal from heartbreak. Why? Well, we're surmising that maybe they invest more emotionally so it takes a little longer to put the pieces back together, but in any case, a guy just out of a relationship may not be the best commitment prospect. Another possibility, at least for some men, is that they are putting up a good front—hiding their feelings, even from themselves—but they are actually just as broken up over it as the woman. Therefore, we would suggest you do a little sleuthing and get more information about his relationship and breakup. How long were they together? What ended it? Who ended it? Why does he think he's ready to date again? What is he looking for that he and his ex didn't have in their relationship? These are all questions you want to ask this guy on a date (though it might be a little forward on a first date, so play it cool and ask these questions over a number of dates, but eventually you will want to know all the answers).

Also keep in mind that the biggest risk of dating this guy is that very frequently the new love in a recently broken-up guy's life ends up being the "transition girl" and not the "forever girl." While we'd love it if you were the case to prove this wrong, we're just pointing it out because our job here is to protect your heart and commitment goals as best we can.

Mr. Separated-but-not-yet-Divorced

Similar to the above just-out-of-a-relationship scenario, this Disaster includes a whole additional layer of complications. Not only do you need to find out if Mr. Separated is ready to date again, you also need to find out if there is any chance of reconciliation before you throw your heart in the ring—or it may get smashed if he goes back to his wife.

Though still "technically" unavailable, we're putting this one in a different category because there are cases where the man is actually legally separated and heading toward divorce. But again, are you just the rebound chick? Can you handle it if you are? Also, how far along is the divorce? Has it been filed? Is this something you're willing to wait for while he works out not only the legal ramifications but also any left-over emotional baggage he needs to process?

Mr. Separated might think he's totally ready to dive into another relationship only to have a massive freak-out when the paperwork starts getting close to being done—especially if he thinks that you're somehow expecting him to commit as soon as the documents are signed. He may have been able to commit once but then gets a new case of vulnera-phobia with an "I don't want to make the same mistake again" twist. You might be nothing like his ex, but that doesn't mean the thoughts won't still enter his mind, even if only subconsciously, as the finalization gets close.

And then there is Mr. Not-So-Separated. The guy who tells you he's separated but is separated only in his own mind, as his wife hasn't been a part of this internal discussion. He's the one who keeps his ring in his pocket until he's pulling out his keys to walk in the door of his house. He's a much bigger risk.

Sadly, there seems to be many definitions of "separated" out there. To whatever degree your potential mate may be separated, you need to be wary that this is a commitment-risky proposition to take on. There are many variables that could thwart the separated man's ability to commit when he finally is available. But realize that even if he is truly separated in the real and legal sense of the word, he's still *not* totally available to you right now because the divorce isn't final so be wary before jumping in too deep.

Mr. Married-to-My-Job

For some men, there is a lot to be gained from their professional status. And the kudos they receive for a job well done may be a highlight of their life. But the man who can't remember what it's like to relax outside of the office or the one who is so committed to success and excelling that he doesn't have time for much else, well, you can see how it might eventually be a problem getting him to pay attention to you.

Fostering a close relationship requires some time investment, some nurturing of the connection, and some focus on the two of you. If a man is a workaholic, he may be powerful and smart and interesting, but if you never see him, would that make you happy? Some women think they're willing to sacrifice close connection for the prestige that a successful workaholic might give them by association. However, think about what you really want in a committed relationship. Are you looking for someone to financially support you, or are you looking for someone who will be there with you?

This Disaster may seem okay up front until you start feeling neglected because he never has time for you; he's always working on the weekends and continues the late hours even though he doesn't really have to. A committed relationship is called a partnership for a reason. Make sure that the workaholic man you're seeing understands that you need to be a priority as much as his power position. If you're not, you will have to decide if this is something you can live with. But be aware: He may not be available to you when you really need him.

Mr. My-History-Could-Be-a-Problem

We'll be the first ones to say that people sometimes deserve second (and even third) chances in life, and that a man can certainly overcome a difficult set of circumstances in his past to grow into a very worthy and committed present partner. That said, there are definitely some situations that should put you on red alert if you've set a committed long-term relationship as a goal.

A guy's history can give you important clues to his character. For example, if you discover he's a quitter or has a history of running when the going gets tough—like he dropped out of college not because he wasn't smart enough, but because he couldn't handle the amount of work—it could indicate a man who also might quit a relationship if it reaches a point where it is too stressful for him to handle. Accordingly, you can probably imagine why that would be a bad trait for a long-term partnership since undoubtedly there are going to be some "for worse" moments along with the better in any relationship.

Another scenario? If you find out he's had a string of long relationships that he hasn't stuck with for one reason or another and the excuses he gives for their demise don't really seem sound to you. Again, you're looking at someone whose personal history shows vulnera-phobia or some other issue that prevents him from making the move toward forever. An additional flag in his dating history could be if he's never had a relationship over three weeks and he's, say, thirty-five years old. Do we really have to explain that one at this point? He's vulnera-phobic—to the max.

What we're trying to impart is that judgment of a person's past is not something we advocate, especially if he has risen above it, but if he has a characteristic that seems to indicate some kind of non-commitment-friendly inclination, it would be prudent to take note.

Mr. Mentally-Unstable-Addict

Right now you're probably thinking, *Of course I'm not going to date some guy with mental issues or serious addictions.* To that we counter, you just might be surprised. Addictions and psychological conditions don't usually show up on a first date—or even a second, third, or sometimes twentieth date—you might actually wind up in a relationship with a man with an underlying psychological problem without even knowing it.

Issues like compulsive gambling, alcoholism, and drug use will probably show up on your radar sooner than other things. But don't forget that there are low-grade addictions that can affect a relationship as well like Internet addictions (be it porn, Scrabble, or online dating). Or, sometimes a guy may think he has something controlled but after a while his will-power wears off and he can no longer keep it under wraps—or he gets comfortable around you and his true colors start to shine through.

Whatever the case, this can be a tough road to hoe. This is especially true if he's not willing to admit he has a problem, or if he's too embarrassed to do so for fear of losing you or appearing vulnerable.

Take, for example, Heather, whose boyfriend's issues didn't show up until they were well into a serious relationship:

Mike and I had had a nearly perfect relationship for about a year. Things were going great. We were inseparable and had a fabulous time together. Though I'd noticed that he did exhibit some compulsive behaviors, like he would work out all the time or spend a lot of money on things he really didn't need. I figured it was okay because as a result his body looked great and he had a good job so it was his hard-earned money to spend. However, then other troubling traits started to surface. He got increasingly moody and it was becoming really difficult, if not impossible, to please him. He also started to be very demanding of me sexually. Some sort of disturbing things that hadn't happened before in the bedroom started becoming increasingly prevalent. It was disconcerting.

Finally, I discovered some text messages on his phone and e-mails on his computer that proved my worst fears true. He had a serious sexual addiction. When I called him out on the issue, he made excuses for his behavior, tried to blame some of it on me, and said things to my face that I knew were outright lies. I gave him as many chances as I could but in the end had to leave him even though I loved him because I knew that I was looking for something long term and couldn't be with someone who put his compulsions before my well-being. Not to mention that I couldn't handle being with someone whom I could never be sure wasn't cheating on me!

As tough as it was for Heather, she did the right thing. Trying to compete with an addiction for affection is a losing battle if the man doesn't see it as a problem, or if he does admit to a compulsion but isn't willing to do anything about it. And even if the situation isn't one where the man might cheat on you with another woman, keep in mind that he will in essence "cheat" on you with whatever his issue/addiction is because it will eventually become more important to him than you if it's not addressed. Choosing to be with someone with this kind of personality is definitely a poor commitment risk.

What's more, consider that if he *does* agree to get help/change and wants to fight for the relationship, it may still be a bumpy road. Rachel's story is case in point:

Sometimes I don't understand why I ever met Scott. I think that my life would have taken a very different, less complicated turn if we hadn't been connected by the universe. But I made my choice to be with this man and I'm sticking to it. However, it's not been easy. You see, I discovered Scott's drinking problem when we were dating. As a result, I broke off our relationship and told him I couldn't put myself into that kind of situation. However, Scott actually stepped up to the plate as opposed to many guys with addictions who run. Scott wanted to change his life. Wanted to be with me. Wanted to earn my trust back. So, I hung in there and he got sober and we got back together.

Eventually we married and we've been together for eight years in a solid relationship. However, now instead of his alcoholism, we deal with the depression and other elements of his addictive personality on a daily basis. I made my choice; I stuck by him and do love him, but I will tell women looking for a long-term relationship that if they decide to stay with a man who exhibits these kinds of traits, it's not always going to be an easy life. Even if he treats the clearly manifested problem, it may surface in other areas in the future.

If you're looking for a commitment, realize that a man with issues may eventually be able to commit to you, but there will always be another entity in your relationship—whatever it is that he has to suppress or deal with on a daily basis. And in the end, this may make him not wholly available to you because a part of him will always be tied up in that fight. This doesn't mean you shouldn't love him; it just means you have to be aware of what you're getting yourself into.

The Safety Clause

One last important thing to consider is why you might be attracted to an unavailable man. Does it somehow feel safer because you don't have to deal with commitment? You don't have to worry about him committing if it's not even a possibility.

There is also the issue that many women love: He's a project—a man who is troubled, but who a woman thinks she can fix. Are you one of those women? We warn against that. With a little dash of tough love, we suggest that a better route toward future happiness and commitment is to look for a man who doesn't need to have something rectified before he can be yours.

This leads us to the crux of our next chapter's discussion: Not only must your guy be available to commit to you; *you* must also be available to commit to *him*. We know, you probably think you're ready—but are you absolutely, 100 percent sure?

THE COMMITMENT-READY MAN ... Makes himself

truly available and willing to commit to you. Dating someone who is married, separated, or otherwise unavailable is a gamble. Occasionally it works, but more often than not it doesn't. If you enter into any high-risk relationship, you must be prepared for an uphill battle.

COMMITMENT
Means You're Ready to Commit Too!

So you've heard that men can smell desperation a mile away. Well, guess what? They can also smell "I'm not ready to commit just yet but you're fun" a mile away too. And if a potentially commitment-ready man is picking up signs that you're not into him in a long-term kind of way, a commitment right now is not gonna happen—even if you think you might want it at some point down the road.

Why? Well, in order for a committed relationship to work, both parties must be ready and available to commit to each other. Yes, that means you too! Interestingly, while stereotypes of male commitment-phobia have been woven into every sphere of pop culture, making it seem like all men are more prone to being relationship sprinters instead of marathoners, more and more women are now sprinting. The result? A lot of guys are left scratching their heads wondering, *What's up with that?*

Often female commitment-phobia stems from some of the same reasons it does for men: a nagging suspicion that somehow, somewhere, there's a better partner out there; she's just not ready; she's still enjoying having fun with good-looking guys and the hot sex. Or, she has her own commitment issues based on family experiences or past relationship experiences, just like men, as we will discuss later.

There is another important development factoring heavily into the commitment equation: Society's view of how a woman should live her life has loosened up within the past fifteen years. Salaries for women have increased in many professions, more women than men appear to be excelling academically, and females have permanently established themselves as career oriented. These career advancements have provided financial liberation for women, allowing them to purchase their own apartments and cars, and luxury goods. Women now live a self-sufficient lifestyle unheard of two generations ago. They also have a sexual liberty unparalleled in modern society. This coupled with the fact that women are also able to conceive later, thanks to modern medical advances, means that some of the pressure to find a husband while still young has been alleviated. What's more, some women are not desirous of having children, sooner or even later.

But, we're probably not telling you anything here you didn't already know. After all, you're a female living in these times. What we are trying to impart, however, is that sometimes you aren't aware that the thing keeping you from commitment is *you*.

Vulnera-Phobia Role Reversal

Women want commitment. Whether or not it's true, people (especially men) assume that any woman throwing her hat and heart into the dating ring is looking for that other type of ring that sparkles. And the truth is, many if not most women do want that, at least at some point. As do the majority of men—eventually, which we've discussed in earlier chapters. That said, many women today take the time to enjoy the single life before taking that walk down the aisle. With more opportunity open to them, the white picket fence is not as attractive as a shot at the corner office.

It's fabulous that today's modern woman has opportunities that past generations could never even have entertained. A recent study by *Cosmopolitan* magazine found that almost one-third of women today (31 percent) are ultra-modern females who believe that women can do everything men can and, in some cases, more. Of the people polled, 74 percent said women are equally or more likely to do better than men in the workplace. And relationship-wise, this group of women will date, fall in love, and have fun with guys, but only marry if it's right. In fact, 71 percent would rather never be married than marry and later divorce.

But, at the same time, this plethora of potentials can lead to commitment confusion. Women are now told that they can have it all, so they start to think they should wait to commit until everything is perfect. That means the right man, the right timing, the right financial situation, the right connection. Problem is, that can lead to a lot of Mr. Right Now situations without a woman even realizing that Mr. Right Now might actually be a terrific Mr. Forever. But since her focus is split thanks to all these other distractions, she might actually miss the "real thing" without even knowing it. With all the other options coming at her, it can be difficult to decide when, if, and with whom commitment should happen.

There is also the possibility, however, that a woman is masking her fear of commitment by making her life impenetrably busy. Keep in mind that vulnera-phobia can wear many faces. A single girl might say, "Well, I just don't have time for a serious relationship with everything else I've got going on in my life." And while that might be true, busyness is also an incredibly potent device for intimacy avoidance. While women typically are socialized to handle feelings of vulnerability better than men, it doesn't necessarily mean they like feeling that way or won't go to extraordinary lengths to avoid it. This may also be a more prevalent reaction if a gal has had her heart crushed a few times.

Another possible root of a woman's vulnera-phobia is what she may have learned from the female role models in her life. If her mother gave up her career to raise a family, or perhaps never even got to explore her career interests, the daughter may have subconsciously come to believe that having a committed relationship is the equivalent of sacrificing everything that is self-defining about her life as a single woman. In other words, as soon as she meets a guy and settles down, her days of being successful are over—or at least that's the message she's somehow internalized. Instead of realizing that a healthy relationship could work to push her even further in her career, since personal happiness often translates into professional success, the vulnera-phobic woman fears that a serious relationship will spell career suicide. It is therefore likely that the female vulnera-phobe will avoid anything but casual dating. And even though on the surface she may lament the lack of available guys, it's actually her fears that are helping to keep men at arm's length.

How so? Well, feeling confused and at bay, the guys who are looking for more than a good time don't know how to read women's intentions anymore. They may find themselves wondering, *Is she dating because she's looking to forge a future with me or only because she wants to have fun? We had sex on the first date: does that mean she's really into me or that she's not serious about anything long lasting?* Ironically, a variation of these questions is likely what you've been wrestling with.

In fact, some of the guys who are looking for real lifelong commitment have concluded that financially self-sufficient, upscale career women aren't interested in marriage, particularly if having children is not a priority. They wonder, *Why do they need me?* The answer, to their dismay, is that a woman really no longer *needs* a man—and this role reversal is showing no signs of letting up.

....

Role Reversal

Consider the commitment quandary of Neil, thirty-four years old, who is actually looking for something more than a fling, as often happens as guys mature and the vulnera-phobia begins to wane:

> *I've wanted to settle down for a while now, but the women I've dated are too interested in their careers, want a casual lover for fun and passing companionship, or are simply too scared of the commitment levels required to live with someone. It seems to me, women just aren't ready to compromise their growing independence and are very frightened of commitment. I dated a couple of girls I was crazy about and would have settled down with. Every time I attempted to deepen the relationship, bring it to a new level of commitment, it was the girl who panicked and backed off.*

You see, once the thrill of being a player has worn thin, most men start to think about finding a Miss Right to make their Mrs., but the type of woman they're going to be attracted to at that point is likely successful, smart, attractive, and . . . the kind of woman who has possibly given up on finding a man to keep up with her. Some of these women have in fact become so cynical in the process that they've actually been converted to players just as men are turning in their team jerseys. As one woman in her mid-thirties boasted:

After wasting years in go-nowhere relationships and mourning my aging eggs, I have come to terms with the whole motherhood thing. I am now happy to admit I am not obsessed with the tick, tick of my biological clock. Sour grapes? Probably initially, but not anymore. I am also no longer panicked about not getting married. If I decide to have children, I have more options than merely seeking a stable semi-permanent relationship. A guy can be replaced by a fertility clinic, and that has to be less anxiety provoking than my former self being consumed by the dating scene.

....

While we absolutely applaud any woman who is comfortable with her independence, we also want to point out that this kind of attitude may hold back a successful woman from even trying to meet someone special anymore. And much to her surprise, when she reaches that point of "not caring," her acceptance of her single status may actually make her more attractive to many men. In other words, don't let an "I'm-single-and-fabulous" mantra prevent you from keeping your eyes open to the beauty of a committed relationship should it present itself.

He Is, She Isn't
Another interesting situation comes up for many "I'm-finally-ready-for-more" men when trying to broach the subject of exclusivity with a vulnera-phobic woman. Usually

what happens in this case is that they've been out on a few dates, are very interested, and would like to date monogamously. But as soon as the initial step or conversation is initiated to put them on the road to "this is serious," they are disappointed to find that their dream partner isn't receptive to dating them and them alone.

....

The Boy Toy Option

Bobby, thirty-four, is a smart, personable, good-looking pharmaceutical representative who recently found himself in such a situation after a serious attempt at Internet dating.

> One woman I dated recently was very lusty and great in the sack. She kidded me about coming over and making a service call. She was incredibly sexy, but otherwise kept me at arm's length until I began to feel unsure of myself. Imagine a woman doing this to a guy and you'll have a good sense of what I was feeling. Still, we had amazing sexual chemistry and in the midst of one lovemaking session, I joked, "Am I your boy toy?"
>
> She said, "What if you really are?" I was at once flattered and insulted. "Is that all we're about?" I challenged. She fractured my commitment desires when she told me she was dating someone else. I told her, "I can't really date you and know that you're having sex with some other guy." She said she wasn't ready to settle down and was just doing what a lot of guys do, and what I probably have done in the past. I couldn't deny that. I said, "If that's what you're up to, I'm going to play it that way. I'll continue to come over, get laid, and date other women until I find The One;

that's where I am." She looked at me, smiled wryly, and said, "Cool, sounds great!"

Maybe I'm just old-fashioned, but a woman wanting to date and get down with two guys—or maybe more—is kind of off-putting. It's not that I think women should be prudes; it's that I want a relationship and want a woman who does, too.

....

Basically, Bobby may have encountered one of the 16 percent of the women in that *Cosmopolitan* study who labeled themselves "Pleasure Seekers"—women who believe life is too short not to enjoy every second. And 55 percent of this group think it's fine to have relationships that are just about sex. Basically, the point we're making is that there are women out there who aren't commitment minded. When they find a man who is, they're not doing the female population any favors by keeping him otherwise engaged, thus preventing him from finding a woman who wants something more.

But guys do this all the time, stringing women along with no plans for commitment. You're right, many do. But, do you really want to be like one of the guys in that case? We're guessing "no," as you're assumedly reading this book in search of commitment clues, but part of our goal here is also to wake up any woman who might be fooling herself. Playing the field does not realistically go hand-in-hand with a finding a long-term relationship.

You also have to remember that men are animals and still possess primal instincts even as a more evolved species. One of these instincts is that a man can sense when a woman is only looking for a good time or when she is seeking something more. Call it a vibe or intuition, but men can definitely pick up on this distinction. Realize though, we're not telling you to play coy or act a certain way to trap a man. We are, however, trying to get you to be honest with yourself, with him, and with your goals. Behavioral acts will eventually be figured out. If you're only looking for a good time, that's fine. But don't convince yourself otherwise if that's where you're at right now in your relationship journey. There are no rules, but there is always self-awareness, honesty, and integrity. And yes, timing is frequently everything. But you can't force your clocks to synchronize.

Self-Sabotage

While female empowerment and pop culture may have something to do with a woman's decision to skirt commitment, it might actually be her real life that has her talking herself out of relationships. And goodness knows we understand why—after enough heartbreaks and hard knocks in the love department, it's enough to make any woman give up. However, there are still good men out there and a woman who truly wants a commitment can find one, but she needs to make sure she's not thwarting her own efforts if that's her goal.

How so? Well, keep in mind that it is very easy to undermine a relationship. And women are actually very skilled self-saboteurs when they set their mind—conscious or unconscious—to it. Whether they are actually suffering from vulnera-phobia themselves (which means they hit the three-month mark in a relationship and start looking for the escape hatch) or do it right before the wedding, there is a sizable minority of women who are interested in the party, not the aftermath. For example, do you remember the recent runaway bride who took off on a cross-country road trip in a premarital panic? She eventually came around (at least for a while), but the point is, many others don't, and they don't make headlines either.

For some women, reaching the level where their meaningful connection is turning into commitment can be simply terrifying. In fact, some of those women are the ones complaining about the epidemic of commitment-phobic men. Are you one of them? Check out some of the most common types of self-saboteurs:

The Whiner: She complains that all the good guys are taken and that she always ends up with leftovers and ne'er-do-wells. What she doesn't admit is that she has a talent for picking losers or noncommitters who basically give her an excuse for avoiding commitment. Her favorite lament is that relationships don't work—and she makes sure that her prophecy is self-fulfilled by consistently choosing the wrong kind of man, or at the very least, a seriously vulnera-phobic one. And two vulnera-phobes together don't stand a chance in hell of developing anything that will last for the long term.

The Junkie: She acts like he's an addictive substance. Rather than move on, she breaks up, goes into withdrawal, and then returns to him and the same failing relationship . . . sometimes over and over and over again. She's too caught up in the revolving door with the same noncommittal guy to get involved with someone who is actually available. Instead, she'd rather keep returning and get her fix, but just like a drug, it's never enough and willpower alone won't break the addiction.

The Perfectionist: No matter how terrific he is, she's convinced that the next guy will be even better. He'll be more successful, better looking, more fun, better in bed, just more and better than whatever she has at present. If he's 80 percent of what she wants, her mantra is why settle for less than 100 percent? Underlying this commitment avoidance is a variation of Gloria Steinem's famous statement, "A woman needs a man like a fish needs a bicycle." The Perfectionist is looking around for a bicycle, but she wants one that will win the Tour de France.

The Critic: Closely related to the Perfectionist, she is more vocal about her impossible standards. She finds a commitment-ready guy with all the right stuff and tears him into little pieces. She measures him against an unrealistic fantasy: he's not tall enough, or fit enough, or rich enough, or sexy enough. Whatever doesn't measure up, she verges on being obsessive in pointing it out to him until it drives him away, because as you'll remember, a guy is not looking to be put down; he's looking to be built up. If he doesn't feel adequate around her, why on earth would he risk being vulnerable around her too?

The Wild Child: Some girls just wanna have fun. If it's good for guys, why not girls? Maybe they don't have the monogamous gene, or maybe they fear being trapped in a traditional marriage with the burden of a husband and children with little room for personal growth. Whatever the case, they enjoy sexual variety and their plans for settling down, like their male counterparts, are some years away.

The Speed Dater: These women would shack up with a guy instantly if they truly felt there was a future—but they're not willing to let relationships grow over time; they want that click right away. They want to fall head over heels instantly. If they don't, they write the guy off without a second chance.

What this type is forgetting is that sometimes love happens on date three or four.

The Walking Wounded: They have had a rash of bad relationships and feel hammered by the dating experience. As a result, they can't even entertain the idea of trying again. Putting their heart on the line one more time might just kill them, or at least that is what they have convinced themselves. These women could also be dealing with past familial wounds that keep them from seeking commitment, as they fear playing out the dynamics of their own dysfunctional family experience.

The Stereotypical Escape Artist: These women self-sabotage as an attempt to avoid the plight of their mothers. They've watched their mothers struggle to maintain a balance between family, self, and career—with both their sense of self and their careers being placed on the back burner time and again to make room for the obligations they had to their family. The reality of it is that this was expected of their mothers and it is not expected of them. But it's often hard for today's woman to recognize that distinction, so she panics and flees before she can get saddled with even more responsibility.

Recognize yourself in any of these types? If so, you may be unwittingly undermining your own chances for commitment. Keep in mind that a guy dealing with any of the previous types is going to experience many of the same thoughts, worries, and upsets that a woman facing a vulnera-phobic man experiences. He may find himself wondering if the fact that she is dating others points to a lack of loyalty or a flighty heart. Maybe she will be forever loyal once she makes her decision, or she may just be a woman who will never be able to be true to one man. And even though it is a clear double standard, guys have less tolerance for a woman who is sleeping with other lovers. They want to be the only one, especially when they are edging toward being ready to commit.

If a man is a secure individual and not prone to attacks of paranoia, he may be able to cope with such uncertainty; if not, he will constantly be second-guessing her and trying to find out where she is, what she's doing, and with whom. This type of worry and anxiety can, of course, leave him exhausted and make her resent him, which ultimately isn't good for any relationship. And it definitely doesn't bode well for commitment.

Hope for Relationship Recovery

If you think you might be sabotaging your own attempts at finding a future with a man, don't fret. It's not too late to change your tune and get back on track. Here are some things you can do to help you find your way back to relationship central; these suggestions are likely to put you in a more monogamous, male-friendly frame of mind.

Hang out with happy couples. There is something to be said about positive relationship role models. If you're down on love, forget feeling like a third wheel and instead embrace chances to hang out with some of your happily coupled friends. It'll remind you what a healthy and sane relationship looks like and can renew your faith in the idea that there are commitment-worthy men out there. Or, if you're a tad vulnera-phobic yourself, it can help reassure you that a good relationship can add to your life in positive ways.

Spend time with your male friends. Think all men suck? Well, what about your nice straight guy friends to whom you're not attracted (or so you've always said) but whose company you enjoy? Do they suck too? Maybe not. Even if they aren't guys you'd want to date, it would benefit you to remind yourself that there are nice men out there who are deserving of your company and vice versa. Not all guys are jerks or vulnera-phobes. Just because you don't want to date your set of guy friends doesn't mean they can't help restore your faith in men.

Make a list of things you like about being in a relationship. So you've decided you're totally fine being single—no really, *totally* fine. But even if you are this happy with your single status, it's not a bad exercise to remind yourself of the things you actually enjoy about having a steady relationship. It will not only help you realize that you are ready to get out there and look for Mr. Right, but it might also help you identify where you are in the commitment scheme. If the only thing you write down is sex, you're in a different place than the person that says she wants companionship and connection as well.

Look at online dating sites. Even if online dating isn't your thing, just perusing some of the sites is a great reminder that there is more than one fish in the sea. This is especially helpful if you're hung up on a toxic guy to whom you keep returning, or you've decided all the good ones are taken. Just one quick spin on the Web and you can see how many men really are still out there. And one of them might possibly be looking for you. So, when you're ready to give up completely, go male Internet shopping. It's a terrific way to restore hope that somewhere out there the right match for you is still waiting to be discovered.

Another thing to keep in mind is that men like women who display some vulnerability. However, that vulnerability, like many other things, is good in a modest amount, but bad in excess. Still, if you've developed a rock-hard shell to prevent commitment hopes from creeping in and possibly hurting you, don't be afraid to soften it up a little.

The bottom line: In order for a long-term relationship to really happen, both the man and the woman are going to have to take a risk and find themselves naked—literally and emotionally. The good news, though, is that once both parties are willing to risk being a little vulnerable with each other, they'll be on their way to something real, because commitment is about sticking with it through the good, the bad, and the ugly, which will be covered in the next chapter.

THE COMMITMENT-READY MAN ... Will only commit if he thinks the woman he is with truly desires a commitment with *him*. Be careful that your aspirations or even past hurts are not impeding your progress toward a commitment and unwittingly giving off the wrong vibe. If a commitment is your goal, make sure he knows how important he is in your life.

COMMITMENT
Is Being There

*F*ight or flight? That is the question. When it comes to commitment, all the other components we've discussed thus far are critical. But there is one that absolutely cannot be overlooked: Will he be there when it counts?

We don't mean just showing up. Physical presence is important, but we're also talking unmitigated emotional support. We're talking investment in your well-being. We're talking sticking it out when things get sticky. We're talking staying together—for better or for worse. A man who is ready to commit will be there through thick and thin. A guy who disappears when he knows his girlfriend has her period, either because she's hormonal or not interested in sex, is making a statement: He won't be there when things get rougher than PMS either.

When you think about finding the person you want to spend the rest of your life with, you think about someone who will be your companion, lover, and friend, right? It's the idea of finding a rock to help keep you grounded in the ebb and flow of life. But if that rock is porous, it will float away with the first tidal wave that hits—or even the first high tide.

The point is, when it comes to commitment, being there is a non-negotiable. Because what good is a partner who will just float away? With that in mind, it pays to consider what constitutes "being there" and the realities that go hand-in-hand with being together forever.

When the Going Gets Tough

When the going gets tough, the tough stay put. Or at least the committed do. No doubt that when relationship issues become a little less than fabulous it can ratchet up a guy's vulnera-phobia big time. In those first idyllic months when everything is wonderful and new in a relationship, it's easier to deal with any real-life struggles as they creep up because the love drug helps mask whatever imperfections may surface. But once that initial high wanes a bit, that's when future relationship potential may really be assessed.

The true test of commitment is not when everything is roses and candlelight. It's actually when things are strained or challenging that the reality of the strength of a partners' connection sets in. Maturity means forming a long-lasting bond with the unique, very human, and imperfect person you've chosen. It means focusing on the long-term promise rather than the short-term foibles, which seem larger and larger as an individual gets more and more scared.

This idea is very important when it comes to determining the probability of a relationship lasting. It's something that we have affectionately come to call "The Pimple Principle."

The Pimple Principle

Let's say that someone you are talking to has a huge zit on his face, but you don't even notice it because you are concentrating on the person as a whole. But, as soon as the person points it out or you notice its prominence during closer inspection, it's suddenly the only thing you can see. That's the Pimple Principle: When a little blemish on a person suddenly takes on way more importance than it should ever have been given.

When signs of the Pimple Principle begin to show up, however, it's time to take notice. As soon as a guy starts to get scared about a relationship, he starts being less accepting of your smaller blemishes. The little things he overlooked initially begin to get magnified. Before the Pimple Principle is active, your tendency to run late and keep him waiting while he watches you dress is sexy. When the Pimple Principle activates, he's threatening to leave without you. Before the Pimple Principle, he finds your quirks charming. After a flare-up, he starts to find them annoying.

So, is this a clue that you need commitment Clearasil? Not necessarily. It could be that he's panicking and looking for a reason to exit, but keep in mind that it might be a sign of something else. Before you similarly panic, pay attention first to what his complaints are and examine their validity. Ask yourself the following:

Is he criticizing me personally or my behavior? Little pot-shots and putdowns are not cool. You don't need that. Relationships are tough enough without being made to feel less than adequate for something that might be perfectly normal but is suddenly wearing on his nerves.

Is his criticism constructive and ringing true, or unfounded and petty? This is where a judgment call may be in order. Look at what kinds of pimples he's pointing out. If the criticisms are about an issue a little more involved than you always being five minutes late or leaving the top off the peanut butter jar, it's worth looking at, at least to ascertain if he has a point. If, however, he's pointing out a bunch of stupid, silly little things, then he might be in a full-blown vulneraphobic state.

Are his complaints necessary and legitimate and, consequently, should be addressed? Both partners need to be able to bring up things that might be concerning them without fear that the other person will get defensive and angry if the complaints are real and could affect the relationship. If the complaints are red herrings, before you write them off as nitpicking consider the fact that they may also be indicative of a larger underlying issue that should be examined. Also, how you deal with criticism as a couple (giving and receiving) can definitely determine your long-term viability.

So what should you do if you think the Pimple Principle has actually set in? Well, here's what you don't do: obsess. That'll make everything worse and might lead to a full-blown case of "acne" as you start freaking out and behaving weird, which will give him even more pimples to spot. Instead, treat the blemish as a guy would: Get proactive! Remember, guys are action oriented. So, in this case, you need to meet him on his level. Ask him what's going on and listen to what he has to say. Does he have a point? You might even ask a trusted girlfriend if what he's saying resonates with what she knows about your personality.

A man who gets stuck in the Pimple Principle mentality, however, is probably not going to be a man who will support you when something more pressing than a small blemish appears. This is important to find out early. What happens if you end up together for the long term and something really major goes down? You want someone who can handle crises by your side, not someone who says, "Wow, this is too much. I'm out of here!"

Is there a way to assess if he'll stick it out? Well, like with most things, the true test takes place when it happens. However, there are a few little clues that a guy will be there when it counts. Keep in mind that when the going gets tough, a man can start to feel very vulnerable. The man who has commitment on his mind, however, is the one who's not afraid to stare down his feelings of vulnerability when the road is bumpy. Here are a few signs that your man knows what it means to be there:

If you two have had an argument, is he ever the one who will initiate the reconciliation? Admitting he was wrong means he's comfortable showing you that he's vulnerable. The guy who is able to go away, think about a fight, and then own up to his culpability is a guy who recognizes what it means to be part of a team. This is a man who will likely stick it out, because not only does he not want to lose you over something stupid he did or said, but he also is willing to step up and rectify the situation.

If you have a medical issue, or even a falling-out with a girlfriend, is he there for you, listening with concern, or offering to be there for you? How does he handle your tears? Men by and large are uncomfortable with weepy women. However, if he's willing to hold you, listen to you, and cares enough to be there when you're emotional, even if it makes him uncomfortable to see you hurting or sad—this is a man who gets that sometimes your needs are larger than his own vulnerable feelings. He's able to put his fears on hold long enough to help you with yours. That is *definitely* being there.

If *he* has a medical issue, or any other serious concern, will he reach out to you for help, or will he deal with it himself and perhaps (or maybe not) tell you about it afterward? Guys don't want to appear anything less than manly, so typically if he has an issue, he might just try to take care of it himself or ignore it. Why? Again, because he fears looking vulnerable. However, if he opens up about it and is willing to ask for your support, he is okay with accepting his weaknesses and understands that you want to be there for him as well. That is a good sign that he understands the meaning of a through-thick-and-thin partnership.

Being there means not only being physically present—which can be an issue for some male character types like "the workaholic" or "the sports junkie" who are wrapped up in other things. It also suggests a willingness to accept the vulnerability that goes along with being emotionally invested in someone else. Worrying about another person's well-being adds yet another responsibility to life. A commitment-ready man is ready to take on the task. A commitment-ready man will show up when things are good and when disaster strikes. A commitment-ready man understands that his life is now about more than just himself. It's about you too—or you two.

Soul Mate Versus Settling

Of course, no woman wants to lower her standards to accept a partner who is less than her ideal, and we are definitely not advocating that. But this book would be incomplete without some discussion of the wide range between I'm-desperate-and-ready settling and I've-found-a-great-match success.

Call it the Hollywood Syndrome, but today, more and more people than ever before are holding out for that classic romantic movie happy ending. Unfortunately, the continual quest for that perfect soul mate may actually thwart one's chances of coupled-up happiness. How so? Well, an individual may have shot after shot at a great relationship and still be thinking, *But this isn't how it happened for Julia Roberts or Richard Gere in* Pretty Woman. Well, guess what? That's not how it happened for those two in real life either. They've both had their share of ups and downs in relationships, and none of them were perfect or easy.

The problem is that while waiting for the perfect Mr. or Miss Right to show up a lot of people pass on what might have been a wonderful, fulfilling relationship with incredible long-term potential just because they didn't think the person was absolutely everything they had on their wish list. While the idea of a soul mate is hugely romantic—and more power to the people who think they've found theirs—our fear is that what it's really about is setting the bar so high that no one can get over it. In fact, the typical dater, male or female, looking for a soul mate is usually too much of a perfectionist; there is no match that is made in heaven. The result? There are a lot of lonely people out there who missed out on a potentially very good life while searching for the ultimate life.

What does this have to do with commitment and being there? Well, to begin with, saying you're holding out for your soul mate is a very clever way of masking vulnera-phobia. Men and women use this one equally well to hide their fear of commitment. For a guy wooing a potential new flame, however, all he has to say is "Well, she just wasn't my soul mate" and he can get himself out of any conversation as to why his last relationship didn't work out. Is that the truth? Maybe. Or is it a cop-out? Most likely. This is a man who has not spent time figuring out what he really wants, or accepting that he's not going to find a neurosurgeon Playboy Playmate of the Year with a heart of gold.

If a guy is adamantly on the hunt for his soul mate and he's not saying you're it, do you *really* think commitment is around the corner? Of course, he's not going to mention it if he doesn't (especially if he's getting you into bed), but you may be able to ascertain his feelings on this issue through his use of the term. You can even probe the guy you're dating a little bit. An easy way to do that, keeping within our romantic movie theme, is to bring up a movie where the main pair clearly embodies the cinema soul mate ideal, like *The Notebook*, *When Harry Met Sally*, or *Atonement*. One little conversation about those movies and you can at least get an idea if your guy thinks soul mates are possible or just a bunch of Hollywood hooey.

The man constantly in search of his soul mate might be a little more of a commitment risk. Why? Men are natural-born one-uppers. If there's a possibility of upgrading what he already has for something better, he'll likely think: *Bring it on!* So even if you're ultimately his perfect match, he may find himself wondering if you're really as good as it gets. It's a bit of a Neanderthal mentality, but it really does happen.

But don't put all the blame on him. This form of commitment escape is even more prevalent among women—who are frequently taken with romantic books and movies—and yes, the underlying issue is the same as it is for men, vulneraphobia. What the "I'm waiting for the romance novel storyline" type of thinking does for women, however, is support avoidance of making a commitment to Mr. Almost Right. In fact, when the heat abates in a relationship, we're all a Mr. or Miss Almost Right. Sure, some may be closer than others, but the bottom line is, nobody's perfect. So, finding the perfect soul mate should not be the objective if commitment is your goal.

A better plan would be to look for a partner with compatible interests, who is not empathetically challenged, who has compatible values and life goals, and with whom you have good chemistry. And it doesn't hurt if both of you have the ability to push back personal boundaries so that you evolve personally—the mutual growth factor goes a long way to combat boredom. Also very important is having an openness that results in sharing your internal life with each other. Basically, it should be about finding the person who best meshes with you and who also wants to be there for you.

The unrealistic aspect of soul mate, the "I don't want to settle" element, has kept many a person from being open to what could be a very good relationship, even though it is not comparable to some movie screen image. Again, there is a wide gap between settling and finding the perfect life companion. Both extremes are not likely to work.

Also keep in mind that after the love-struck period every couple has a reality check: The initial infatuation has worn off and they see their partner in a more realistic light. Some Hollywood movies seem to focus on the front end—the honeymoon period—but the real work begins when the illusion ends and you move into the back end—or reality. This is where the term *soul mate* messes people up. Anyone can seem like your soul mate when you're in the first throes of mad adoration. The person who is actually your soul mate is more likely the one who is still there when he's seen you after a bout with the stomach flu, or after you've had a blowout fight. A true soul mate is the kind who stays for the sake of the relationship, not the one who bolts as soon as things start pointing toward something a little less than, well, the perfect Hollywood ending.

THE COMMITMENT-READY MAN ... Realizes he's willing to labor through hard times as long as he has you by his side. When he starts putting your well-being and your relationship above other commitments in his life, he'll likely realize that he's able to commit because he *wants* to be there, through thick and thin. Why? Quite simply, he can no longer imagine his life any other way.

Afterword

Stay Strong

So, you've reached the end of this book and you are still waiting for the fairy tale. While we truly hope that Prince Charming happens for you sooner rather than later, we also must impart that life doesn't usually unfold like a childhood story. Unfortunately, the path to the castle may be mired with obstacles, and you'll probably have to kiss a lot of frogs along the way before finding your true prince. And sometimes even when you think you've found him and all the signs are pointing toward commitment, the rug will get pulled out and you'll be left lying on your back staring at the ceiling and wondering what the heck just happened—which ironically was the case for Kimberly, who had her heart smashed into a million little pieces during the time we were writing this book.

With that in mind, what can one do in order to temper the ups and downs of the quest for a happily-ever-after ending? Short of a magic wand or a fairy godmother, your next best bet is to learn to develop a healthy sense of dating resilience. To begin with, nix the "what did I do wrong" thinking. Women tend to blame themselves when things don't work out the way they'd envisioned. They wonder what they could have done better, how they might have affected a more positive outcome, and why they weren't enough for him.

But, guess what? You are enough. *More* than enough. Don't doubt that. Instead, focus on getting through the relationship maze with your self-respect and self-regard intact. Here are some final tips for learning to adapt and bounce back while navigating the slippery slope toward finding a real man willing to commit.

Keep hope alive. You can't change the fact that stuff happens—Mr. Right stops returning your calls and turns out to be Mr. Very Wrong—but you can change how you interpret and respond to these events. If you're rejected, don't make it about yourself, and avoid telling yourself that a setback is forever. Try visualizing what you want, rather than worrying about what you don't have.

Accept that rejection is a part of living. Don't get caught up in "What's wrong with me?" Chances are the reason is him and his commitment issues. And, if it's simply not a good fit for him at this time in his male maturation process, that's about his preference, not a report card on you.

Pace yourself and stay in the game. Do your best to continue with the journey. When you have a setback, rather than withdrawing, take decisive actions; review your plan, research new avenues for meeting men and for enriching your friendship network. This is a way to step back, to rest, and to re-energize while still staying open to possibility.

Stay involved. Do something regularly, like going to the gym, pursuing a hobby, or hanging out with your friends to avoid obsessing about the stress of dating. Ask yourself, *What's one* *thing I can accomplish today that helps me feel good and recharges my spirit?* Then go ahead and build your agenda from that point.

Nurture a positive view of yourself. Developing confidence in your ability to stay the course and trusting your instincts helps foster resilience. Knowing what you deserve will hone your ability to believe that you are worthy of a great, committed relationship.

Build your support group. Many studies show that an important factor in resilience is having a responsive network of family and friends. Relationships that nurture and offer encouragement are a definite boon when it comes time for you to bounce back from another Mr. Wrong and even when you are just trying not to lose hope that Mr. Right is out there. In other words, keep that circle around you, because you'll need them to weather the ups and the downs.

Stay alert for self-discovery opportunities. In the midst of the dating struggle is an opportunity to learn something about yourself; you may find that you have grown in some respect as a result of the journey. Many people who have experienced difficulties have reported a greater sense of strength even while feeling vulnerable.

Practice self-love. Pay attention to your own needs and feelings. Treat your body well. Taking care of yourself will help keep your mind and body primed to deal with situations that require resilience.

Bottom line: You need some degree of dating resilience if you are to complete the trip intact. But even with that, heartbreak may litter your journey toward Mr. Right. You need to heed the red flags, but you also need to be patient. It's a tricky balancing act, and the guidelines we've provided are intended to stack the odds in favor of commitment, but maintaining realistic expectations is also vital.

Do keep in mind that men are slower to commit than women. Their hesitance involves vulnera-phobia and all the other things that we've discussed, but it should also be mentioned that men want to be absolutely, positively sure they are making the right decision—which definitely extends their commitment timeline. And given that it's women who initiate nearly two-thirds of all divorces, it seems that once men *do* commit to marriage, many intend to be in it for the long haul. So pay attention to the clues, but also realize that each journey to commitment is going to be unique—for you and for him.

Finally, we have one more important thought to leave you with: Love simply cannot always be controlled by reason. If it could, there wouldn't be so many songs about breakups and dashed dreams. We are not robots that can be instantly programmed or deprogrammed depending on the situation. To think that you can stop being in love with someone simply because you should is naive at best, and it is only possible if you don't really feel that strongly about the person to begin with.

So, go forth, love well, and, by all means, try to find that fairy tale. We only hope that along the way you'll keep in mind the advice we've offered, so that your story writes itself with the best possible outcome for you.

Appendix A

The Real Reasons Checklist

*Y*ou've read through the book and now you know how to identify a vulnera-phobic male, but keep this quick checklist in mind when you're trying to decide if he's commitment ready. You don't have to have all of them marked, but the more you can check off, the better you'll know if he's "The One"—and what you have to work on in order to make commitment happen.

❑ He happily makes room for you in his life and his home. He says "we" a lot.

❑ He asks your opinion about major things going on in his life, like how to approach his boss about a much-deserved promotion or when to take vacation time.

❑ He tells his ex, if they are still amicable or share ties like children, that he has a wonderful new woman in his life.

❑ He takes your relationship public to his family, coworkers, and friends.

❑ He volunteers information like who was on the phone, how much he makes, and problems he may be having.

❑ He's passionate and loving and wants to be around you as much as possible.

❑ He's responsive to your requests and meets your needs willingly and consistently.

❑ He takes responsibility for his actions and doesn't make you utter the phrase "It's okay, I understand" all the time.

❑ He starts *behaving* in a fashion consistent to the role of boyfriend/fiancé/partner (meaning that his actions support his words, his mannerisms back up his proclamations of love).

❑ He has a sincere desire to please you and make you happy, not just a desire to satisfy his own needs (the latter may indicate he's in it more for sex than commitment).

❑ He isn't afraid to share his feelings with you (which is a huge vulnerability risk) and be honest about his emotions.

❑ He is supportive and complimentary of you. A man who is super critical of you or others may have unrealistic expectations of what he'll find in a long-term relationship.

❏ He has a strong set of standards or beliefs by which he lives. A committed man knows the meaning of morality and loyalty.

❏ He doesn't shoot down the concept of marriage outright, nor does he sound cynical about the high divorce rate or condone his friend's extramarital affairs (no matter how hot the mistress may be).

❏ He isn't motivated solely by a desire to obtain personal pleasure for himself (true hedonists have trouble committing).

❏ He understands the meaning of compromise and doesn't expect you to do all the bending and accommodating in the relationship.

❏ He recognizes that he can be independent and in a relationship at the same time.

❏ He's comfortable and not threatened when you go out with other couples. In fact, he enjoys it and the idea of couplehood.

❏ He is respectful when you're out together and doesn't ogle or flirt unnecessarily with other women when you're together (or when you're apart for that matter).

❏ He isn't caught up with the idea of finding a "perfect" soul mate (i.e. neurosurgeon Playboy bunny who does comedy on the weekends). Instead, he has a realistic view of what he wants in a partner.

The Top Ten Reasons Sex Is Not Commitment

We live in a different world today. Years ago, no one had sex prior to marriage (or if they did, they were looked upon poorly). Today, practically everyone has some sexual experience before walking down the aisle. In fact, most people want to know if they're sexually compatible prior to saying, "I do." But this change in societal acceptance has also affected how sex is viewed. Many women, though contemporary in their thought, still want to believe that if they sleep with a man, it's some kind of sign of commitment. Here are some reasons to keep in mind that suggest sex alone is not enough to sustain a long-term relationship, that sex doesn't have the same meaning and implication that it had in the past.

1. Sex before marriage is commonplace.

As we've mentioned, people are doing it. And a wedding ring is not usually involved in most people's first sexual experience in this day and age. Because sex is more available and engaged in without the old "rules of engagement," sex alone doesn't make a contemporary commitment.

2. More people are having sex thanks to the prevalence of birth control.

The thought of an unwanted pregnancy used to be enough to keep people abstaining. Today, however, you can get condoms, pills, rings, shots and implants to prevent an unplanned pregnancy from happening. Studies highlighting the rise in sexual activity correspond with the increasing number of contraception options, illustrating the fact that this new freedom also means more people have more partners in their sexual lives.

3. Women have discovered their sexual selves.

No longer complacent in the bedroom, like the perfect '50s housewife stereotype, women are now allowed to enjoy and even *want* sex! And it doesn't make her a slut if she likes it! That said, however, it's opened up the pool of people having sex, and though many women want a commitment out of a sexual relationship, that's not always the case. More women are having sex like men today—which means when and where they want it!

4. Cyberspace has facilitated hooking up.

Feeling horny? Click here. Seriously, there are so many options for people right at their fingertips today that almost anyone can find sexual satisfaction online if they really want it. Problem is, sometimes there are too many choices, and so if one sexual partner doesn't work out, a click of the mouse can lead to another option.

5. Sexual experimentation is more openly discussed.

Thanks to shows like HBO's *Real Sex* documentaries, fetishes and toys and other things that would never have been discussed except behind closed-doors are now out in the wide open and on cable TV. You might want sex to be a commitment, but it could also be someone's experiment...food for thought!

6. Sex isn't viewed as a significant relationship statement.

Men (perhaps even more than today's contemporary women) don't regard sex as signifying a statement of commitment. In fact, for most men sex may be lower on the commitment ladder than a host of other behaviors—integrating you into his friendship network, meeting his family, or sharing his most personal feelings.

7. Sexual attraction that is *too* strong may lead to a relationship burn out.

In the complexity of factors that are suggestive of commitment, sexual attraction is only one of many. Similar interests and life goals, the "friendship factor," and compatible personality factors are at least equally important. A strong sexual attraction sometimes may overshadow a deficiency in these other factors, leading to a "crush crash" on the road to the altar.

8. Sex can actually come back to bite you.

Yes, the double standard is still alive, if not as robust as it was in years past. For some men, the thought, *she was easy with me, is she easy with other guys also, will she be trustworthy?* is haunting. This isn't to suggest refraining, just to consider that while he comes on to you and is thrilled with your affirmative response, he may have second thoughts. In other words, not only is sex *not* a reliable indicator of commitment, sometimes it ends up being a deterrent!

9. Sex can leave you chemically confused.

You know you've felt it. You're on the fence about some guy and then you have sex and suddenly you're in love. Your rational self has just taken a back seat to oxytocin, the love chemical. Just getting a little closer (or really, really close as it may be in this case) will spike all these feel-good hormones in your body and his. So you may be thinking Mr. Right Now is actually Mr. Right purely because of the chemical reactions going on in your body. And he might think it too…in that moment. But give it sufficient time because those chemicals wane. It is what is left when the sexual after-buzz wears off that determines commitment, not the post-coital confusion.

10. Sex is sometimes just sport.

Like it or not, sometimes sex is just sex. It can be recreation for some people. Just because you're working up a sweat and burning calories à deux doesn't mean that there is any emotional attachment involved. This goes for both sexes, but especially men who can seemingly disassociate their sexual pleasure from the body next to them more readily than the female set. But it does go both ways (think "Samantha" from *Sex and the City*). Just keep in mind that a roll in the hay does not equal a trip down the aisle. If you can't handle that reality, you probably shouldn't be having sex.

Appendix C

How to Find a Commitment-Ready Man in Cyberspace

*Y*ou might meet *him* in a bar. You might meet *him* in the supermarket. You might meet *him* through a friend of a friend. But really, in this day and age, you stand a good chance of meeting *him* online.

Cyberdating has ditched its stigma. It used to be that people thought of any kind of matchmaking as for the desperate spinster set. *Au contraire.* Today online dating has become one of the most efficient and popular ways of finding a mate. According to a Pew Institute and American Life Project online dating survey, 15 percent of American adults—30 million people—say they know someone who has been in a long-term relationship or married someone he or she met online.

The advantages are many and the results are often much longer lasting than some random person you met while downing alcohol. Remember, knowledge is power for any woman trying to level the dating playing field, and online dating can help a woman see who might be worth dating and who is still playing the field. With that in mind, we decided cyberdating was worth an exploration with a focus on how your computer keyboard could connect you with your Mr. Right.

How Online Dating Can Help You Connect

Here's the deal: In order to meet Mr. Right, you have to meet more men. We know, you're thinking: *But there aren't any good ones left.* Sorry to bust your pity-bubble. Just log onto the Internet. According to *U.S. News & World Report*, of the 87 million single people in the United States, over 40 million users visit online dating sites each year—that's about half the number of single adults in the United States. And millions report they have found true love.

So, step one in any successful online connection process is to go to a few Web dating sites for no other reason than to dispel the notion that there are no single men left. Why? Well, hope is an important part of the finding Mr. Right process. If you lose hope, then you're probably going to lose attractiveness too. This is because men can read desperation a mile away (and it's not pretty).

So, go ahead, just take a peek at an online dating site (your choice, but easy ones to start with might include *Match.com*, Yahoo Personals, or *JDate.com*). It's time to see what is out there. Now you're curious.

Still struggling to get over the idea of being on an online dating site? Consider these additional reasons why online dating may just be the ONLY way to date in the near future.

A supermarket-sized selection! Can you imagine how many parties you'd have to frequent in order to meet the thousands of men you can see posted online? You'd be flat-out exhausted and would have to give up your full-time job in order to make searching for Mr. Right your career instead. With online dating, however, you can significantly expand your dating pool with just the click of a mouse button. In fact, according to a *Match.com* study, two-thirds of single adults view online relationship sites as an effective way to meet many potential dates.

No more questioning: "Is he single or is he gay?" Face it. If you're out at a bar, club, movie, or wherever and you see a hot guy, you are probably going to wonder if he's married and if he is playing for yours or the other team. So, then you're going to do that awkward I've-got-to-get-a-peek-at-his-left-hand maneuver to see if there is a ring. And even if his ring-finger is without adornment, you can't be sure if he's straight or not. Though online dating doesn't take away all risk of meeting men who are sexually confused or pretending to be single, it does help minimize the uncomfortable fact-finding mission that happens when you're out and trying to glean the same info. If he's online and single, he's actually looking!

It allows for quick fact finding. There is *no* way at a bar or a coffee house that you could within seconds find out some guy's income potential, marital status, height, weight, feelings about children, religious views, educational background, and more. However, online you can do just that. *But people embellish online* you argue? And they don't at happy hour? Cyberdating gets a lot of the specifics out of the way fast so you can decide if this is someone with whom you might match up or not within seconds of reading a profile. Think of it as preference-centered dating.

It gives you time to find out more (like running a background check). A few e-mails back-and-forth with a potential date and perhaps a phone conversation and you will probably have a full name of the person you're possibly meeting for coffee. If so, hello Google (not that we always recommend doing a Google search on your dates, but if you have *any* questions or a nagging feeling they're not telling the truth, hit up Google and save yourself the time investment or heartache later). If you don't get a full name or are against searching out your date's specs on the net, then at the very least you'll have had enough interaction so that you might feel more confident about meeting up in person.

It is highly efficient. Maybe it seems depersonalizing, but think about it, convenience talks. We live in a world of PDAs, cell phones, computers, and so on. Everything around us is programmed for efficiency. Therefore, is it really so bad if dating follows suit? We're not talking the entire process of dating—we certainly don't want anyone taking the romance out of it—just the meet-and-greet phase. You've heard the saying that dating is a numbers game. Well, up your number and it might soon be game over for you (in a good way, as in you've found *him*).

With all these positives encircling cyberdating, we hope you are running out of reasons *not* to try it. Now we can move on to the ways to spot a worthy man in your cyberdating searches.

Posting, Perusing, and Pursuing

Okay, so you've seen the light and you are now open to online dating (or you already were but you are now ready for the next step).

Posting
First of all, post a profile of yourself. A few words to the wise here however. There are certain things you can do with

your profile that will help you attract a commitment-ready man and others that will score you a player.

Photo Posting

One of the biggest things to keep in mind when posting is that men are visual. So, your pictures are going to be worth a thousand words. Write a killer profile but post a bad photo and you can bet you won't get as many responses because many men won't even read what you wrote before clicking "next."

But here's where the *big* item comes in. You may be tempted to post some really sexy shot of yourself (come on, who doesn't want to look *hot*), but keep in mind if you make your photo ops too sultry or show too much skin, you're also going to get a lot of responses from "good time guys." In other words, you may get a commitment-ready man to respond to that as well, but you'll be so deluged with e-mails from men writing with something else on the brain you likely won't be able to differentiate the keepers from the players (or it will be harder).

In this same vein, there is really no point in putting up a photo that doesn't look like you at this very moment in time. That doesn't mean you can't put up a gorgeous photo of yourself (as you should since this is the first impression your potential date will have of you), but you need to make sure it's a look you can replicate if you were to meet Mr. Right for coffee . . . today. Keep these ideas in mind when posting a great photo to try and attract the kind of commitment-ready man you're seeking:

1. **Do smile for the camera.** Being mysterious and coy may work in a bar, but online your best bet is to look friendly and fun. Post a happy, smiling photo!
2. **Don't wear sunglasses, a hat, or anything that obstructs.** You want to show your beautiful smile,

sparkling eyes, and lovely hair. Any photo that disguises those is a wasted upload!

3. **Do dress cute and casual.** You want to look like you're at Sunday brunch with friends, or like you're on a first date. You want to look like a "real" person a potential date could imagine hanging out with!

4. **Don't try to be too sexy.** Keep cleavage shots and micro-miniskirts to a minimum. And bedroom eyes should stay in the bedroom. Trashy is not going to get you the kind of responses you're seeking.

5. **Do include action shots.** No, not you flying through the air, but yes, you doing something that you love. This shows potential dates about your interests without you saying a word!

6. **Do leave something to the imagination.** No matter how great you look in a bikini, don't post it. Guys like having a little something left to discover about you!

7. **Do vary outfits, poses, and backgrounds.** Remember, you're trying to create a well-rounded picture collage of yourself from all angles.

8. **Don't post an "aged" photo of yourself.** Seriously, they will notice the ten-year age difference when you walk in the door.

9. **Do include a close-up.** This is especially important for your main photo. If all your photos are from a distance, you'll likely be kept at a distance as well.

10. **Do post a full-body shot!** If you don't post a full-body shot, most men assume you're hiding something—whether true or not!

11. **Don't post group photos.** You want his focus to remain on you, not your best friend who happens to be cute, bubbly, and blond!

12. ***Don't* post a photo minus your ex.** Seriously, people can see that area where you "erased" the other person in the photo and all that's left is his arm around you.

13. ***Don't* post a pet photo.** Unless you're completely devoted to Mittens or Fido and it's a cute picture of you playing with them, leave your little pals off your profile. You don't want to be seen as that lonely woman with all the cats do you?

14. ***Don't* post a photo with children.** If you have kids, you probably love them to death and that's great, but do you really want to expose them to all the people who will view your photos? And if they're not *your* children, do you want to have to explain this in your profile?

15. ***Don't* post meaningless photos.** If you have five landscape photos, three pictures of your favorite television stars, and two photos of yourself . . . you're likely to get lost in the mix. Remember, you should be the star of your profile. If a guy is perusing your pix, it's because he wants to know what you look like. So while occasionally including a photo of your favorite piece of artwork might be a good jumping off point for future conversations, chances are the response will be more direct if you're standing in front of that piece of art looking cute and interested. Keep all eyes on you . . . where they belong!

Text Posting

It is also important to craft a profile that is reflective of the *real* you if you're hoping to find your real Mr. Right. This is the first time you get to "speak" to your prospective dates. You want to keep things upbeat. This is not the place to weed out people you might not be interested in, nor is it the space to list the fact that you "don't really know why you're online" or are "sick of the bar scene." It might be true, but why waste profile space on something that doesn't further your quest to find a match? Instead, focus on giving someone reading your profile a picture of who you are, and why he would be lucky to know you!

Highlight your hobbies. Go ahead and mention your quirky skills—that's fun and different. For example, you might get responses if you are a champion Frisbee thrower or can sit on the bottom of the pool for 5 minutes. But also be sure to list some interests that are more mainstream, such as restaurants you frequent, books you couldn't put down, bands that get you revved. Remember, potential dates will also be looking for common "chatting" ground!

Don't be afraid to use humor. After "attractive," men almost always state they're seeking a woman with a sense of humor. But don't just say you have it, show it. One genuinely clever profile moment could net you many future dates.

Minimize any "gold-digging" words. You may think it's harmless to mention that you enjoy the finer things in life, fancy restaurants, exotic trips, the best wines . . . but in man-speak a potential date might take that to mean you're only interested in the size of his wallet.

Be confident. Men can sniff out "needy" or "insecure" miles away. You've got lots to offer the right match for you so play up your strengths!

Keep your "What I'm seeking" essay short! Listing twenty things you're looking for in a man could lower his self-image if he only matches four items on that list. Remember, you're trying to encourage him to write! Everyone wants someone honest, good-looking, fun, and intelligent, so leave those out and put in something more meaningful. Like, "I tend to be a little serious, so my ideal match would know how to convince me stay in bed on Sunday morning instead of leaping up to head to the gym!"

Don't write your life story. While you are usually given a significant amount of words to get your point across, keep in mind that people have short attention spans these days. You want to catch his attention, give him enough information to make him want to know more, but leave him something to wonder about and some questions to ask you!

Personalize, personalize, personalize. Remember, you are trying to explain what makes you unique. The key is to give enough description that someone reading your profile can picture a date with you and all the fun you'll have.

Hold off on mentioning the C word. Commitment! Obviously you want it or you wouldn't still be reading this book. And he might too. But mentioning it too early in a profile can read as "desperate to find a match now" and that is seldom seen as attractive. Same thing goes for the "kiddie" factor. Keep your biological clock on vibrate until you've at least met!

Perusing the Scene

Once your "I'm looking for Mr. Right" profile is posted and giving off the correct messages (that you're looking for more than a hookup), it's time to do a little searching on your own. This is the "cruising" phase of cyberdating.

Some women sit back and wait to see who finds them, but the most successful online daters also go in search of Mr. Right. Taking a proactive stance will net you even more results, and it's empowering because you're not sitting around hoping something will happen. You're making it happen. When looking for a commitment-ready man online, however, keep these things in mind:

Mix it up. Most online sites have all kinds of searches you can do. There is usually one main search where you can plug in the specs you're looking for and see what the computer orders up for you. But don't forget to check other areas like "Mutual Matches," "Reverse Matches," or "Who's Viewed Me." There might be someone the computer finds for you that is also looking for your type, or perhaps someone who is a little shy and unwilling to make the first e-mail initiative but who keeps checking out your profile. By trying all the different searches, you may uncover a needle in a haystack.

Vary your criteria. One thing to keep in mind is it's important to be willing to vary the criteria you cite for potential dates a little. Everyone will have their deal-breakers (like smoking habits or perhaps religious affiliations) and those should stay intact. However, if you are willing to tinker with the things that are less vital to you in a match (eye color, hair color, job description), you might come up with somebody great! If after a while Prince Charming hasn't stopped by, simply change a few fields and key words to see if it gives you a new range of prospects.

Search and search again. The frequent searcher is often the one that finds a new posting first. In other words, you snooze, you lose. Some awesome guy may have been thinking about posting his profile for a while and then does so only to get snapped up by some other woman first. Don't slack . . . be on the lookout for any new members that might intrigue you (at the very least do a broad search every few days).

So, you've got the searching thing down and you find someone of interest. Time to do a commitment-ready check. Here are a list of sections on his profile that you should examine. Remember, nothing is set in stone and there could always be exceptions to any rule. But on the whole, look at these areas of a profile to assess his sincerity about finding "the one."

- **Photos**—Does he have pictures of himself with other women on the site (and we're not talking his mom here)? Does he have lots of half-naked photos of himself posted ("Look at my ripped chest")? Is his ex-girlfriend clearly cut out of the photos he's posted? This is a player red flag. You can get a sense of a guy's intentions by which photos he posts.
- **Status**—Does his "status" say "single" in the "I'm truly available" sense of the word? Remember, sometimes "separated" can mean "separated but forgot to tell my wife." Look really closely for clues in the text accompanying any questionable status statements.
- **Children**—If his "Wants children" box on his profile is a "No way" or "Maybe someday" he's obviously in a different place than a man who checks "Yes, definitely."
- **Seeking**—Does he say he's looking for a "long-term relationship" or does he make mention of "short-term relationship" or "play." Obviously guys with the latter on their profile are open to well . . . remember our section on sex isn't commitment? If not, go back and reread immediately.

Pursuing the Dream Guy

Okay, so he "passed" and doesn't seem to be a complete vulnera-phobic or player from what you can tell. Then feel free to send an e-mail to him. Creative e-mails definitely get more responses. You don't have to go crazy, but there are definitely Dos and Don'ts when it comes to sending a prospect that all important first note. Here are some tricks to make the most of your cyber-communication skills:

1. **Do choose a clever subject line.** Aside from your *Username*, this is the first communication he'll see from you. Catchy titles sometimes determine if your e-mail gets read! It's great if you can link it to something you read in their profile. Don't try to be too cutesy though . . . there is a fine line.

2. **Do mention what they wrote.** Just a sentence or two about why you found them intriguing is usually enough. This shows you paid attention . . . and actually read the profile!

3. **Do give compliments.** You know you like to hear them—what makes you think guys are any different? Here's a tip. Guys LOVE compliments. Notice his blue eyes, great physique, engaging smile, obvious sense of humor, whatever! Don't be afraid to let him know that you found it appealing. Everyone likes to hear good things about themselves!

4. **Don't be too sarcastic.** Remember that in e-mail communication, the other person doesn't have the luxury of hearing your vocal inflection. Therefore, you might be kidding, but it could be misconstrued. Better to save that kind of playfulness for later.

5. **Do ask questions!** This is a way to encourage a response from someone. Pretend you're having a con-

versation in person. Say "What do you think about X, Y, Z" or "Have you ever been to . . . ?" to keep the other person interested . . . and writing you back.

6. **Don't be too coy.** Think you're being mysterious or alluring? Chances are it just comes across as "I don't like you" in an e-mail. Friendly and fun is a better tone to use than hard-to-get (literally and figuratively).

7. **Do notice similarities.** If you both have a shared interest, point it out! Say something like "I can't believe you adore going to the Zoo on the weekend, so do I!" or "You mentioned loving classical music. Someday I should tell you about my extensive collection." By bringing focus to what you have in common he will think "Hey, maybe we would have something to chat about?"

8. **Do give a few details.** If there is something you'd like to elaborate on that you weren't comfortable putting in your profile (like your actual profession or where you grew up, for example), this is the place to do it. Just don't get too personal too soon.

9. **Don't write too much initially.** This is meant to make dating easier. Save your time and energy, and don't give away all your secrets in the first e-mail. You want to save tidbits for future conversations!

10. **Do sound positive.** Guys aren't interested in whiners, complainers, or gossipers. You want to leave them with the feeling that getting to know you might be fun!

Skirt Chaser or Commitment Seeker?

What if he's pursuing you? Put his profile through all the tests we outlined above and if you think you might be interested, feel free to write him back. But, here are a couple other red flags to look out for with men online:

How active is he? Usually it is good if you see a profile online where someone has been active recently so you know he's still looking. However, if you see a really hot guy online with a great profile and it's been up for months and he's still active daily . . . ummm . . . chances are he's enjoying the attention a little too much to be serious with you at this point.

Is he fun, fun, fun? Seriously, profiles that are all about "Having a good time no matter what" are usually not the men who are thinking about settling down. There may be exceptions (it's predicated on how it's worded) but . . . just watch out for the guy who is too much fun.

Sometimes boys lie. Just like you thought for a minute about changing your age or your body status ("athletic" can mean carrying a few extra pounds . . . right? NOT!), men do it too. So, keep in mind that if some guy looks too good to be true . . . he might be. A healthy dose of reality in online dating and a dash of skepticism can sometimes serve you well. If all else fails, listen to your gut . . . it'll usually steer you in the right direction.

Don't Share Your Privates

One last thing before we turn you loose on the Internet . . . safety first. *Always!* That means you don't give out personal information until you're comfortable, and even then keep it to a separate e-mail you use only for online dating or a cell phone where you can screen calls. Never give out your home address.

And when it's time to take your online flirtations out into the real world . . . just remember these tips. Because finding Mr. Right should be fun, not scary.

1. **Do go public.** Choose somewhere populated. You want to make sure there are other people around. And meet at the designated place—it's neutral territory. Don't ever let a date come to your home first!
2. **Do set a time limit.** That way you have a predetermined "out" if you don't gel in person. If, on the other hand, things are going well, you can always extend or schedule another date on the spot!
3. **Do tell a friend where you're going.** And let someone know the name of the person you're meeting (or at the very least, his *Username*), if you can.
4. **Do meet for drinks or coffee only.** You don't want to commit to a meal because it's a lengthier proposition. Let that be your second date if you get along.
5. **Do take a safety call.** Make arrangements to call your friend after the date to let her know you're home. Or have her call during to make sure things are okay. Have a code word to let her know if you're fine or not. And don't worry . . . good guys aren't threatened by this—they know the drill!
6. **Do listen to your instinct.** The majority of guys online are great, so don't be afraid. Be smart, be confident, but *always* trust your instincts!

With all these thoughts in mind, now go turn on your computer and get busy. Mr. Right might be just an e-mail away!

Index

Index

About the Authors

Between them, Joel and Kimberly bring two important perspectives—the man who's an expert on men, and the woman who's been in your shoes (and nearly worn them out). Combined, they have wisdom to share. Their answers are a GPS on the road to commitment.

Joel Block, Ph.D., is an award-winning psychologist who knows the male psyche—not just his; he talks to men all the time. Even more importantly, he specializes in dealing with relationships and sexuality in his very active practice, and he answers dozens of e-mails around the issue of commitment nearly every week. Dr. Block has written nearly twenty books on relationships and sexuality.

You can visit him on the Web at *www.drblock.com*.

Kimberly Dawn Neumann is a popular New York City-based dating/sex/relationship writer who has also worked extensively in the theater (making her privy to more than a little relationship drama). Her work has appeared in such publications as *Cosmopolitan*, *Redbook*, *Marie Claire*, *Maxim*, and more. She and her friends have been in the trenches—some have found true love, others are still looking. But all of them agree that when it comes to commitment, there is a difference between the men that will speak of future and mean it and the boys who are still messing around.

You can visit her on the Web at *www.KDNeumann.com*.